The Bridge Remembered

Edward Coales

The Bridge Remembered

The story of a remarkable hotel in Buttermere

*Do you remember an Inn, Miranda?
Do you remember an Inn?*

Hilaire Belloc

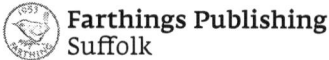
Farthings Publishing
Suffolk

First published in Great Britain 2019
by Farthings Publishing

ISBN 9781798039465

© Edward Coales, 2019

Design and typesetting:
Tam Preston
tampreston.co.uk

Contents

List of Illustrations	VII
Acknowledgements	IX
Foreword	XI
Map of Buttermere	XIII
1. When I Fall in Love	1
2. Far from the Madding Crowd	6
3. First Impressions	14
4. Amateurs in Eden	17
5. It Takes All Sorts	32
6. Food, Glorious Food	43
7. Fun and Games	59
8. Service with a Smile	72
9. A Man for All Reasons	82
10. Over the Hills and Far Away	93
Epilogue	103
Index	107

List Of Illustrations

Map of Buttermere	XIII
The Bridge from the Lorton Road	8
Rodney and Rosemary outside the Bridge	18
Bridge Hotel brochure	22-25
Carrie on Prince with Zoë	30
Visitors' book	33
Rodney and Rosemary in the bar	42
Lunch menu	45
Dorothy and a 'poached' salmon	48

Photograph Album

1. Rodney with Rollo, Zoë and Brandy	51
2. Rodney	52
3. Dorothy and friend with the hotel behind them	53
4. In the kitchen. Pomme, Dorothy and Odilia	53
5. Odilia's 21st birthday	54
6. Local friends of the Twitchins in the bar	54
7. Sketch of Pomme by Zetta	55
8. Rodney returns from serving petrol in the rain	56
9. Sybil and Dorothy	57
10. Sheila, Jane, Vanessa and Brandy	57
11. My Austin Seven – beside Loweswater	58

Chercowski's mug	61
Flame-throwing	65
The staff in 1959	73
Irene and Sybil	74
Bridgettes in high spirits on the footbridge	77
Simon Rocksborough Smith serving petrol	83
Simon burning the hotel rubbish	87
Brandy	94
The Buttermere and Crummock Round	101
John Scadding with the magnum of champagne	102
Rodney and Rosemary relaxing	104

Acknowledgements

Firstly, I would like to thank my wife Sue for all her help and encouragement during the writing and production of this book.

I am highly indebted to Zoë Thomson who has shared with me so many stories about her parents. Zoë's book 'If anything should befall you' has been an invaluable source for my chapter on Rodney and Rosemary's early lives.

I am very grateful to Tam Preston, a professional graphic designer, who designed and typeset the book.

I am also most grateful to all those listed below who have patiently answered all my questions, told me their stories about the Bridge and given me photographs as well as other memorabilia.

Bridge Hotel, Buttermere
Anne Cartmell née Burgess
Tim Cartmell
Sue Coales
Peter Cockshott
Zetta Cowen née Roberts
Eleanor Ella née Stiles
Dorothy Fell
Barbara (Pomme) Frost
Irene Gibson
Marijke Gijswijt née Hofstra
Vanessa Hudson née Ballantyne
John Dixon Hunt
Ann Kyle
Debbi Maurice née Stanley
Oliver (Ollie) Maurice

Christopher Metcalfe-Gibson
John Richardson
Simon Rocksborough Smith
Carrie Ross née Watling
David Ross
Jane Rowe née Cockshott
John Scadding
Heather Shield
Rosa Somerville née Wykes
Alison Steer née Coales
Jen Taylor née Hill
Hugo Thomson
Zoë Thomson née Twitchin
Tilly van Rees née Metcalfe-Gibson
Maud Vickers

Foreword

In May 2009 I stayed at the Bridge Hotel in Buttermere with my wife Sue and my sister Alison Steer. Alison and I had worked at the Bridge in the late fifties and early sixties while we were students, and we had now come to the Lakes to attend Rosemary Twitchin's funeral. Rosemary and her husband Rodney were the owners of the Bridge between 1953 and 1972.

The little church of St Bartholomew's in Loweswater was crowded for the funeral with not only family and friends, but past guests, handymen, waitresses and secretaries. During the service Rosemary's son Rollo, read the poem 'Tarantella' by Hilaire Belloc, which starts with the haunting words, 'Do you remember an Inn, Miranda? Do you remember an Inn?' Could we ever have forgotten the Bridge? Later in the service a past handyman, Simon Rocksborough Smith, gave a wonderful appreciation of Rosemary, that brought back so many happy memories for us all.

Following the burial, we walked up the hill, passing the Kirkstile Inn, to the village hall. Here we listened to story after story about times at the Bridge, which were told with much warmth and affection. Everyone knew that Rodney and Rosemary had run the Bridge Hotel in a very special way.

Later my wife told me that I should record these memories of the Bridge by writing a book about them. At the time I had some other projects in progress, and I forgot about it. However, Sue did not let me forget entirely and in late 2017 I decided to start researching the twenty years that the Twitchins had owned the hotel. I have not made my work any easier by procrastinating for such a long time. Many of the past staff are in their eighties, some were difficult to find and when I did find them their memories were not as sharp as they used to be. Some memories were hazy, and a few were contradictory, so I hope that you will forgive any inaccuracies that you will find in this book. Almost everyone I contacted was incredibly enthusiastic about the idea and they genuinely wanted to share whatever memories they had. Here are their stories, together with an account of the earlier lives of Rodney and Rosemary before they bought the Bridge. I am most grateful to their daughter, Zoë, for allowing me to use some of the research she has done on her family.

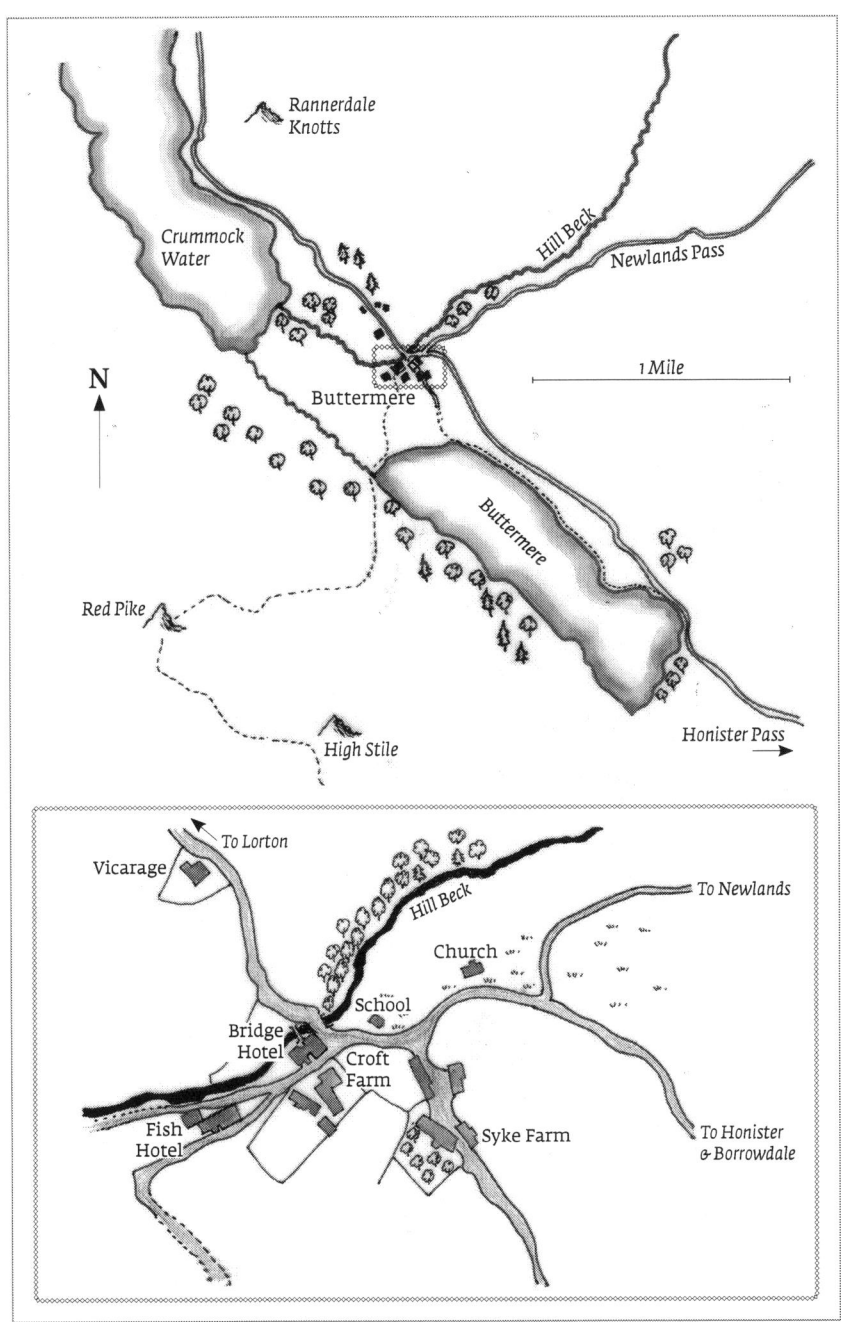

Map showing the Bridge in Buttermere and the wider area

XIII

1

When I Fall in Love

Rodney Archibald Twitchin was born in Byfleet, Surrey in 1915. His father, who was a stockbroker, died suddenly in 1919. Later his mother, with her three small children, moved a few miles south to Shere, and here she ran a guest house to make ends meet. Maybe this is why Rodney, experiencing regular visits from guests coming to stay to be well looked after by his mother, later decided to go into the hotel business. Rodney left school at fifteen and then worked for a firm of discount brokers in the City. He first met Rosemary Cope in 1934 when he was nineteen and she was eighteen. Rosemary, who was born in 1916, was living with her parents in Epsom and studying shorthand and typing. Rodney was immediately smitten by her and he described her as having a gorgeous mass of golden hair, nice blue eyes and an adorable little nose. This delightful young lady was only 5'1" tall, while Rodney stood a foot taller than her at 6'1".

In 1935, no doubt hoping to make his fortune, Rodney sailed to Rangoon to work for the trading company Fairweather, Richards & Co. The relaxing journey on the four-master SS *Derbyshire* took three weeks. Having arrived in Burma he was soon regularly writing to Rosemary and he described his easy colonial life which included playing rugby, rowing, shooting and getting involved in amateur dramatics. He could not resist mentioning to Rosemary that he was also meeting quite a few girls. While Rodney enjoyed the colonial high life, Rosemary wrote that she was also having a busy social life in Surrey, celebrating her 21st birthday in 1937 at the Weybridge tennis club. They wrote to each other fairly often, describing their various experiences in a friendly and chatty way.

In Rangoon Rodney kept failing his language exams, which were required if he was to get promotion and this might have been why he lost his job in 1939. So, he sailed back to England with his tail between his legs on MV *Werdenfels*, a German Hansa Line freighter with six other passengers: three people and three elephants (according to his letter to Rosemary). When Rodney returned, he stayed at his mother's house in Shere. He had little money and no prospects of a job at this point in his life. But he soon got in touch with Rosemary asking to see her again. Around this time Rodney applied to join the Royal Air Force, but, much to his disappointment, he was turned down due to his poor eyesight.

At the outbreak of war Rodney joined the Royal Artillery as a private and he continued to write to Rosemary. Meanwhile Rosemary found a part time secretarial job with the City of London School at Ashtead in Surrey. Later Rosemary's school was evacuated to Keighley in Yorkshire and Rosemary decided to move to Keighley too, so that she could keep her job. Rodney was soon promoted to sergeant in March 1940 and he then moved around several army camps which were mainly in the south of England. Later that year Rodney started officer training and his unit moved to the requisitioned Ullswater Hotel (now called The Inn on the Lake) to be trained in gas warfare. The hotel was situated by the side of Ullswater lake and the surrounding beautiful scenery made a lasting impression on Rodney.

Not everything with the young couple's romance was running smoothly. From the outset Rosemary's father had not approved of Rodney's interest in his daughter. He thought that after the war was over, Rodney would have few prospects of finding a job that would support his daughter in the way that she had been accustomed. There was no family firm to welcome Rodney on his return and he had no qualifications either. Indeed, he described Rodney as hard drinking, certainly not hard working and, perhaps worst of all, he had a fickle nature. Despite all of this, Rodney and

Rosemary did manage to fleetingly meet in Cleethorpes where Rodney was stationed, and they declared their love for each other.

Then in January 1941 Rodney's unit suddenly left on a Cunard liner to an unknown destination. Rosemary immediately started writing to Rodney but her first letters did not reach him until June. Meanwhile Rodney was also writing affectionate letters, but when no letters from Rosemary arrived, he decided to send her a telegram from Durban. It simply said, 'All my love darling'. Unfortunately, what should have a blissful moment for Rosemary, was spoilt by her father hastily opening the telegram before she could intervene. He immediately flew into a rage at the awful thought of Rodney possibly becoming his son in law. Her father's temper, and his dislike for Rodney, did not discourage Rosemary at all. She continued to send Rodney affectionate letters, filled with descriptions of her new job at the Horton Emergency Hospital in Epsom.

Rodney was now in Palestine as a junior officer, where he had joined a battery unit. His letters to Rosemary mentioned marriage as well as Rosemary's father's continuing disapproval of their relationship. Despite this impediment, Rodney plucked up courage and wrote to Rosemary's parents in July 1942 asking their permission for him to be engaged to Rosemary. To the young couple's astonishment and delight Rosemary's father relented and soon the engagement between Mr R A Twitchin and Miss R Cope was announced in The Times.

Not long after this Rodney's unit moved to Egypt to support the battle of El Alemain. By now Rodney had been promoted to Captain. Meanwhile, in their letters to each other Rodney and Rosemary agreed that they would get married as soon as Rodney came home for his first leave. The months dragged on as Rodney's battery, now in Libya, moved around the desert and then, at last, in May 1943, the German and Italian armies surrendered, and the possibility of leave became a wonderful reality.

It was not until November that Rodney was finally given three weeks leave and eventually, he arrived on the SS Amanzora at Greenock on the 9th December. The next day Rodney sent a telegram to Rosemary to say that he was in Scotland, but that she could not expect to see him much before Christmas. What excitement and expectations that must have created! However, only a week later Rodney and Rosemary met in Leatherhead, a 'breathless meeting' as Rodney later described it. He presented her with an engagement ring and asked her to marry him. And so, the frantic arrangements for their wedding started in earnest.

Rodney and Rosemary were married at last in St Martin's church, Epsom on the 29th December with 110 guests. For their honeymoon they spent a night at the Berkeley Hotel before staying a week in Bournemouth. Rosemary then continued to live with her parents and work at the Horton hospital until the end of the war. Meanwhile Rodney's regiment, the 27th Light-Aircraft Artillery, had returned to England where he spent six months training with his battery.

On D-Day, the 6th of June 1944, Rodney was back in action and he found himself in a landing craft trying to reach Gold Beach in Normandy. German strongholds were raking the beach with their guns and overhead a naval bombardment of the German defences added to the dreadful confusion. When he did reach the coast of Normandy, Rodney swiftly drove his jeep out of the landing craft when it promptly sank into the turbulent water and had to be towed on to the beach by a tank. Rodney's engineering skills soon got the jeep started again and, despite a stiff German resistance, he arrived unscathed at Field Marshal Montgomery's headquarters in Creully, near Bayeux the next day.

Later he was promoted to adjutant of his regiment and by the end of the war he had been promoted to Major and he was the Commanding Officer of the Coleraine Battery. Finally, in January 1946 Rodney was demobbed and he returned to Surrey. The happy couple soon bought an attractive house in Woodcote

Close, Epsom where they were at last able to settle down to what proved to be a very happy and successful married life.

Rodney, despite no formal training for a civilian job, soon found a position with Lawley's department store in Regent Street. Meanwhile Rosemary was enjoying a domestic life, maybe feeling that the demanding work she had put in at Horton should give her a well-earned rest. No doubt Rodney felt that life in a department store was not stretching his abilities, because he soon moved to the National Union of Manufacturers where he eventually became the Head of the Export Assistance Department. He was recognised for his hard work by being awarded the MBE in 1952.

It was during these post-war years that Rodney and Rosemary started going up to the Lakes for holidays. They stayed several times at the family-run Scafell Hotel in Rosthwaite, near Keswick, which was owned by a friend, Sandy Badrock. It was not long before they decided that they would like to live in the Lakes to own and run a hotel. They asked Sandy to keep an eye open for any hotels for sale in the area. When they had a message from him in early 1953 to say that the Bridge Hotel in Buttermere was up for sale, they frantically dropped everything they were doing and rushed up to view the hotel. On seeing it for the first time, they fell in love with it and were determined to buy it.

2

Far from the Madding Crowd

Buttermere village lies between the lakes of Buttermere and Crummock Water and is surrounded by the Lake District's Western Fells. It is mostly enclosed by the mountains of Fleetwith Pike, Haystacks, High Crag, High Stile, Red Pike, Robinson and Dale Head. The closeness of these mountains to the lakes creates the most beautiful intense reflections that change in colour throughout the day. As the seasons pass, so the fells around Buttermere also gradually change their subtle pastel shades. These scenes have now made Buttermere and its surrounding landscape a very popular place in the Lake District.

The Buttermere valley has chiefly held its charm due to the National Trust and the fact that it is part of the Lake District National Park which was created in 1951. Before this, in 1934 the National Trust appealed for funds to buy Buttermere lake, Crummock Water and Loweswater and with some later purchases by the Trust, the Buttermere valley is now one of the most protected and unspoilt areas in England.

When Rodney and Rosemary Twitchin first moved to Buttermere in 1953, the village was very much quieter than it is today. The roads from Cockermouth and Keswick into Buttermere village were all very narrow with very few passing places, full of sharp bends and with very steep inclines. The roads were so unnerving to inexperienced travellers that many of them were simply put off from visiting the village. Rodney would advise guests who were arriving at the Bridge for the first time to drive over Newlands Pass. This was shorter than either of the routes over Winlatter Pass or Honister Pass, but it was more narrow and winding for much of its length. The road from the top of Newlands Pass to Buttermere has a steep drop on the right hand-side. New visitors who had arrived in the dark were often horrified when they later saw the road in daylight and remembered how fast they had driven.

Apart from the occasional motor car there was a bus service from Cockermouth twice a day, but the service only ran during the summertime. There was no mains electricity and it was not economical to run a hotel in Buttermere in the wintertime, with so few visitors and such high heating costs. During the winter months life in the village noticeably slowed down as the hotels shut, the tourists disappeared, and it was only the farms that showed any signs of activity.

In 1953, just around the corner from the Bridge, the Folders had dairy cows at Syke Farm and Wilkinsyke Farm and these could be seen in the summertime wending their way through the village twice a day to be milked. Next to the Bridge was Croft Farm, owned by Robbie Jackson and a little further away there was Cragg Farm owned by two Burns sisters. Their other sister, Annie, lived at Wood House. These neighbouring farmers and the other outlying farms all had herds of the small white-faced Herdwick sheep, which are an extremely hardy breed, and to a lesser extent the farmers kept the Yorkshire black-faced Swaledale sheep. Several times a year the sheep would be brought down off the fells to the fields that lie between the two lakes and then the village would become alive with bleating ewes and lambs, barking sheepdogs, shepherds whistling to their dogs and shouting helpers.

There were three hotels in the village in those days. The nearby Fish Hotel was run by Nellie and Chris Greenhow and there was the Buttermere Hotel on the road towards Honister Pass, soon to become a Youth Hostel. The Bridge Hotel, built of stone and slate, was the dominant building in the village. Looking down on the Bridge was the tiny village school that closed in 1953 (now the village room) and the equally tiny Victorian

The Bridge Hotel from the Lorton Road

church. The vicar was Geoffrey White, who lived in the large Victorian vicarage close to the hotel, and who unlike the farmers in his parish, had far fewer sheep in his flock. The nearest policeman was stationed at neighbouring Lorton. Other than the vicarage, the only large house in the centre of the village was Trevene. Due to the very strict planning controls, during the twenty years that the Twitchins kept the Bridge, there was never any new development in the village. Despite all the pressures of tourism, Buttermere still managed to keep its very special charm.

Surprisingly for such a remote and small village, there was a Post Office opposite Cragg Farm with a small shop run by Mary Clark, who opened it eight hours a day, six days a week. Occasionally she helped out at the Bridge. Her husband, Syd, was the road mender or, as he was called locally, the lengthman. He looked after 20 miles of tarmac road that started at the beginning of the B5289 near Low Lorton and ended at the top of Honister Pass. His route also included the road from Buttermere village to the top of Newlands

Pass. His job was to keep the gutters and run-offs clear, repair the dry-stone walls beside the roads, cut back overgrown hedges and even repair potholes with tar and granite chippings. He did this work for thirty-five years, spanning the time the Twitchins were at the Bridge,

Syd was certainly a great character. He was regularly seen in Buttermere, always wearing a cap and smoking his pipe. He was never without his Lakeland terrier, and his bicycle crossbar bristled with his tools. He knew everything about the local weather, the depths and currents of the lakes and if someone unfortunately drowned in one of them, the police always asked Syd where and when the body might turn up. He was a born poacher and a prodigious one. He regularly hooked salmon out of the river Cocker and Maud Vickers, who lives in Lorton, said that any salmon that left the village alive was a very lucky one. Occasionally he would surreptitiously turn up at the Bridge with a large object wrapped in newspaper. Rodney would accept it with alacrity, money would pass hands and the guests would soon enjoy poached salmon for dinner. Syd had a wry sense of humour: Rodney was always driving in a hurry and when Syd saw him approaching, he was known to lie beside the road feigning a heart attack. Rodney would screech to a halt and much to his annoyance, Syd would then stand up, put his pipe in his mouth and saunter off with his bike down the road.

When the Twitchins arrived at the Bridge a few walkers and climbers came to Buttermere and some stayed in the hotels, but they rarely filled them. The tourists mainly came by train to Windermere and Keswick and stayed in well-appointed hotels with their mains electricity and they did not have to move far to enjoy the nearby shops, cafés and restaurants. The Twitchins needed to quickly find new guests who would appreciate the tranquility, the beauty of the scenery and the opportunities for wonderful walking and climbing that Buttermere had to offer. These guests would not come seeking luxury but having once experienced the charm of Buttermere and the welcoming Bridge, the Twitchins hoped that they would want to return.

When I looked into the early history of the Bridge, I found that there were a lot of conflicting dates of ownerships, as well as the various names of the hotel. Therefore, I have not given specific years for its early history.

It is thought that the hotel stands on the site of an 11th century bakery and armoury. Further up the neighbouring beck there was a water mill and these buildings were sold to the church in the early 18th century, which then obtained a beer licence and the Bridge Inn was created. In the 1830's the inn was bought by Jonathan Sleap, and he later renamed it the Victoria Hotel. At some point a Mrs Cooper owned the property and she added the attractive bay windows at the front of the hotel. In the 1880's John Nelson bought and considerably enlarged the hotel, but a review stated, probably euphemistically, that in 1886 the accommodation was very humble and the food, although rough, was wholesome. Perhaps, unsurprisingly, by 1905 it was reported that the hotel was very run down, and it subsequently closed.

Nicholas Size (1866-1953) was an administrator for the railway at Bradford when he bought the derelict Victoria Hotel in the 1920's. He set about renovating and enlarging it to hold around forty guests and he renamed it the Victoria Private Hotel. He also had a vision that Buttermere could be transformed into a village similar to a resort in the Swiss alps. So a large beer garden was proposed behind the hotel with the suggestion of a resident oompah band to give it an Alpine atmosphere. He even proposed to build a chairlift from the village to High Crag (zip wires had not yet been invented); but these ideas never materialised. While developing the hotel Nicholas promoted Buttermere by writing several romantic novels about the village and the surrounding area, set in the 12th century. His best-known novel is

'The Secret Valley', which is about the imagined local resistance to the Norman invaders.

Nicholas Size also created a nine-hole golf course, 1¼ miles in length, that stretched down from the hotel to Crummock Water. The hotel was renamed yet again, this time as the Victoria Golf Hotel. But it was not long before the golf course closed, and the hotel reverted to the Victoria Hotel. Nicholas Size certainly tried to put Buttermere on the map. He encouraged motorists to visit by installing a petrol pump and with foresight he also encouraged walkers to roam the open countryside, much to the irritation of the local landowners.

By 1953 Nicholas Size also owned the Fish Hotel and the Buttermere Hotel but his health was failing and in fact he died later that year. As soon as the Twitchins heard that the Victoria Hotel was for sale they went up to Buttermere and made him an offer, so on the 4th of May 1953 the sale of the hotel was completed.

The Twitchins were now the proud owners of a run-down hotel in a remote area with no mains electricity and no mains water. The hotel's electricity was supplied by a diesel generator, all the water came from the neighbouring beck and the drainage system was extremely doubtful as well. There were only a few bathrooms for the number of bedrooms. Any more bathrooms and the hot water system simply would not have coped. The whole hotel needed decorating, modernising and bringing up to a standard that the Twitchins thought would attract discerning guests. The rooms which were later to be the family flat were deemed to be unsafe because their balconies could have detached themselves from the hotel at any moment. There was much building work to be done, but these improvements could only be done gradually as profits from the business became available.

The Twitchins' young children, Rollo and Zoë, arrived at the Bridge in August 1953. The family started to make the hotel their home, but as the rooms that were to be made into the family flat were being converted, the family had to live in some of the guest rooms at first.

The hotel stood in a dip with the road rising sharply on either side. There was a small wood and a paddock opposite that were owned by the hotel and the beck ran under the road and then beside the hotel. Croft Farm was on the other side of the hotel and a road ran between them down to the Fish Hotel and then there was a track that led down to Buttermere lake. Unfortunately, the position of the Bridge did not offer any splendid views of the lakes, either from the ground floor or the bedrooms. However, with only a short distance down to the shore of Buttermere lake, visitors could soon have the breath-taking views they had come to seek.

The accommodation in the Bridge was not grand. The bedrooms at the front of the house were larger than at the back, two with bay windows, and they all had some form of heating. No bedrooms had en suite bathrooms and there were often queues in the corridors for the bathrooms and latecomers might well be disappointed, finding no hot water all. The rooms at the rear of the hotel were small, some tiny, all with no heating and the corridors were very narrow. At least there were basins in all the rooms. Beds were often jammed against the wall, which made it very difficult for the chambermaids to make the beds. At the beginning of the season the hotel could feel quite cold and the bedrooms remarkably so. On chilly evenings guests could request a hot water bottle to make their beds slightly more comfortable and welcoming. The Twitchins never pretended that the hotel would provide the height of luxury for the guests and the modest tariff reflected this. Very demanding guests were discouraged, and the new owners hoped that their particular style of management would be the main attraction.

The sale agreement included the furnishings, which were extremely dilapidated. Rosemary moved a lot of her family furniture up to the hotel over the years and these included many antiques that gave it a homely as well as an up-market atmosphere. The bedrooms eventually all had good quality paintings or prints on the walls. Rosemary also built up an attractive collection of teapots that adorned the front lounge.

When the Twitchins moved in on the 14th May 1953 (according to the visitors' book now kept in a glass case at the Bridge), the hotel had already opened for the summer at Easter. The new owners had to move fast as the hotel had existing bookings and running the new business must have been an incredibly steep learning curve for them. They had to take over the employment of the local staff and use the existing tradesmen, who might not have been suitable in the Twitchins' opinion. With no experience in the hotel trade at all the Twitchins were in at the deep end, having to suddenly deal with the unfamiliar staff as well as unfamiliar guests with all their different demands and, no doubt, quite a few idiosyncrasies as well.

Once it was clear that the business was a going concern, the hotel was renamed the Bridge Hotel in October 1953 and that is how it has been known ever since.

3

First Impressions

It was a few days before Easter in 1958 that I arrived on an afternoon train at Keswick railway station to start my new job as the handyman at the Bridge Hotel. Typically for the Lake District, the rain was coming down in stair rods and I was greeted by Rodney wearing a long brown and very frayed mackintosh and a wide brimmed hat. He shook my hand enthusiastically, took my case and we dashed to his waiting Austin Sheerline. I had been driven by my father in the Lakes before, who considered himself a fast driver, but I had never been driven as fast as this. With my heart in my mouth, we sped through Newlands, took the hairpin bends at Birk Rigg at full speed and then sailed over Newlands Hause at a cool sixty miles an hour. White-faced sheep perilously loomed in front of us out of the mist and then rapidly scuttled off down the mountainside before we descended into Buttermere. Thankfully we did not meet a single vehicle on our journey.

Having passed the little church perched on a large granite rock, the Bridge Hotel appeared out of the gloom, its grey walls and dark roof glistening in the rain, giving it a somewhat forbidding appearance. We drove over the little stone bridge (hence the name of the hotel) and then swerved left into the hotel car park past two petrol pumps to a screeching halt. Clambering out of the car with unsteady legs, I grabbed my suitcase and quickly followed Rodney. We crossed the little wooden bridge over the beck and then we were in the kitchen where several staff were preparing food in readiness for the first guests that evening. Rodney was immediately showered with questions, 'Can we urgently have more fuel in the Aga as it needs to be hotter for cooking the dinner?' or 'The guest in Room 2 is complaining rather crossly that he hasn't got a plug for the basin.' Patiently he responded to all the queries as well as offering encouragement to the two new female students who were going to help in the kitchen and be waitresses. Meanwhile a bell was ringing in a Wagnerian manner which meant that a passing motorist needed his car filled up with petrol. The two students were now busy laying the dining tables for dinner. I was to be the handyman and there was much to be done as this was the first day of the season.

For three summer holidays before this I had stayed at the Bridge Hotel with my family. As a teenager I enjoyed meeting the other guests and going out with the family for day-long walks or even some rock climbing. I immediately appreciated the beauty of the mountains surrounding the hotel and the easy access to so many challenging summits. As these were my first stays in a hotel, I had no idea whether the hotel was well run or special in any way. But I enjoyed the relaxed atmosphere where everything was done for me and I had a bedroom of my very own with my very own basin. During one of my stays I had dropped a glass into the basin, and it had made a neat hole in the porcelain. I remember having to ashamedly report this to Mr Twitchin, who was remarkably calm and took pains to explain to me that this sort of thing happened on a fairly regular basis and that I, or rather my father, would not be charged for the replacement basin. I thought that he was a very kind and generous man.

My father, John Coales, was a keen rock climber and one afternoon while we were staying at the Bridge, he took me and my younger brother, Martin, to climb the Central Gulley on Great Gable, described as a Moderate climb in the guide book. We arrived much later than planned and with two inexperienced boys aged 13 and 17, the going was very slow. To make matters worse we somehow got on to another climb which we later found was classified as Very Difficult.

The result was that we reached the top of Great Gable at around 9 pm, just as it was getting dark. Now we had to get down. Our returning path to Gatesgarth was four miles long and much of it steep and rocky; a daunting prospect in the dark. With only a feeble torch we gingerly picked our way down towards Windy Gap. It was a very frightening experience and had I known the sheer drops on either side I might well have sat down and refused to move any further. But miraculously we kept to the path and we found ourselves on Scarth Gap at around midnight. My mother, Thea Coales, who had been very worried when we did not turn up for dinner, asked Rodney to raise the alarm when it became dark. So to our relief we could see torches moving up towards us and we were soon met by a team from the Cockermouth Mountain Rescue. They led us down to Gatesgarth and then drove a very tired and traumatised trio back to the Bridge.

Everyone, in the hotel knew that we were missing and most of them had stayed up anxiously waiting for our return. After my mother had tearfully embraced us, Rodney and Rosemary without hesitation opened up the bar. My father announced that it was drinks on him for the rescue team and the drinking lasted into the early hours. I think that was when the Workington Best Bitter ran out. Rodney was a little critical of the venture, but I will always remember his concern and the trouble he took, staying up late waiting, and then celebrating our return. This was typical of his character and his concern for others was the hallmark of his management at the Bridge.

As a rather gauche teenager, I felt that Rodney and Rosemary had gone out of their way to be kind to me on the several occasions I had been staying at the Bridge with my family and I clearly remembered this. So perhaps it was not surprising that as a student in 1958, my Easter holidays found me working as a handyman at the Bridge, callow, somewhat anxious and totally untrained for the duties to come. Yet I was in for a pleasant surprise.

4

Amateurs in Eden

After the Twitchins had taken over the Bridge they worked hard to make the hotel attractive and welcoming for their guests. When you arrived and entered the hall, the first thing you saw was a beautiful flower arrangement by Rosemary. The room was light and airy, there were attractive paintings on the walls, and it was furnished with good antiques. There probably was no one about, but a notice under a frosted glass window told you to ring the bell once for attention. If you did so a benevolent well-spoken gentleman would slide back the window to the office, peering like an owl through his tortoise-shell framed spectacles to greet you. Or it would be a delightful fair-haired lady with a rather posh and husky sounding voice who was equally welcoming. After the formalities a handyman would be summoned to take your luggage to your room and so would start your holiday at the Bridge Hotel, Buttermere under the ownership and management of Rodney and Rosemary Twitchin.

After the initial scramble of moving into the Bridge in 1953, the Twitchins could start to focus on the way they wanted the hotel to be run. They did not want to work to any standard formula; in fact, they did not know a formula to work to, as they both had no formal training in hotel management. So, it was run very much on their own lines. They did try to be highfalutin to start with and they offered a silver service in the dining room, but this required very high standards from waiting staff who needed to be well trained in this exercise. Due to everyone's lack of experience, this was soon discontinued. The decision was made at the outset not to employ any professional hotel staff, other than the cook. There was

Rodney and Rosemary by the hotel front door

a supply of local housewives who were keen to earn extra money and it was an advantage that it was not necessary for them to work full time. Some of the staff were already working at the Bridge and others were chosen who were, it was hoped, scrupulously honest, reliable and extremely loyal. Perhaps Rodney thought that this would not be the case if he employed staff who had worked their way around the hotels in the Lake District.

Because the hotel was only open between Easter and the end of October, Rodney could employ students for the jobs of waitressing (Rodney flippantly called them Bridgettes) as well as handymen. To start with they were nephews and nieces or sons and daughters of close friends. As the years went by many families regularly stayed at the Bridge and the younger members of the family, probably after tasting the delights of evenings in the bar, asked to work at the hotel during a student gap year or during the Easter or summer holidays.

Until they had a secretary some years later, Rosemary did the secretarial work taking the bookings and dealing with the correspondence. Rodney kept a record of all the guests' spending on drinks in the dining room and the bar and completed their bills before they left. He also dealt with the tradesmen's bills which tended to accumulate on a spike and the pile would usually only be investigated when someone complained that they needed to be paid.

Jen Hill, who was secretary from 1965-67, said that there were occasionally complaints about the food or when early morning tea appeared rather too late, probably due to a waitress suffering from a late night. There were even complaints about holes in sheets that Dot or Gladys had failed to notice. But as most guests were already well-known to the Twitchins, these complaints never became an issue and as Jen was on the front desk she would have known if they were. If Jen did receive a complaint, her policy was to make fulsome apologies, and this invariably sorted the matter out.

Rosemary had never cooked seriously in her life as she had nearly always lived at home. Rodney had some experience of fending for himself and he enjoyed cooking and could cook very well. So he liaised with the cook about ordering the food and the menus for the week ahead. Rosemary typed the menus daily for lunch and dinner. In their first year they were encumbered with food rationing and all that that entailed for a hotel, but it thankfully ended the following year.

Rodney had to be up early every morning. He was woken by a member of staff with a mug of tea at 6.30 am. Later Rosemary had breakfast in bed, while combing whichever dog was lying on the bed at the time. After a bacon sandwich and another mug of sweet tea, Rodney would drive off to collect the staff from Cockermouth and Lorton in the green Austin Sheerline limousine. This was nicknamed Tessie after the musical hall singer Tessie O'Shea and her song 'Two ton Tessie'.

In 1958 young Zoë celebrated her birthday by giving a party. I was working as handyman at the time and I was surprised and delighted to be invited. Tessie was filled with a large number of excited children who were collected along the way as Rodney drove us to the Theatre Royal in Workington. The main star of the show that afternoon was none other than the one and only, larger than life, Tessie O'Shea. We settled down in our seats to watch the legendary star. Towards the end of the show she brought the house down by crooning a love song while sensuously stroking the stand of the microphone up and down, watching the audience for its reaction. Rodney in particular was howling with laughter. There was a tea party afterwards and it was not just the children who had smiles on their faces for the rest of the afternoon.

Tessie had a 3,460 cc engine and a voracious appetite for petrol. One morning I was asked by Rodney to drive it to Carlisle on an errand. This was a treat and once on the open road from Cockermouth to Carlisle, I put my foot down and enjoyed the exhilarating experience of such a fine car. There were no blanket speed limits in those days. After completing my errand, I returned with my foot hard down on the accelerator again. Soon there was a splutter, a few jerks and the car coasted to a halt. I had run out of petrol. There was a gallon can of petrol in the car, so I poured it into the tank and continued my journey at the same breakneck speed. To my consternation, precisely eleven miles later, I ran out of petrol again. This time I had to walk a mile to the nearest petrol station and I luckily managed to get a lift back to the abandoned Tessie. Ruefully I drove very sedately back to the Bridge and I managed to reach its petrol pumps without further incident. After Tessie was sold there was a more economical Bedford van with bench seats called Bessie as well as a Mini Traveller.

When anything went wrong Rodney had to leap into action and put it right. Before the electricity came to Buttermere in 1962 there was a Lister generator at the bottom of the garden that had to supply all the hotel's needs. If it went wrong, he desperately tried to fix it, but if that failed, he called out the garage owner, Tom Rawling, from Lorton. The generator had to be filled up with diesel daily and often the batteries needed topping up with sulphuric acid. Once Zoë discovered her father rolling in the beck splashing himself with water. He yelled that he had accidently spilled acid on his trousers and he was trying to wash it off before it did him any harm. Zoë shouted back that it would be far better if he took off his trousers. Rodney exclaimed 'Bloody hell, I'm not letting all the guests see me in my underpants. I would never hear the end of it.'

Buttermere did not have mains water until long after the Twitchins sold the Bridge. The water supply was from the beck that came straight down from the fells, through the wood that was owned by the Twitchins and then it ran beside the hotel. There was an intake some way up in the wood. Rodney would taste the quality of the water every day and if it was dubious, he would go up to the intake and clear it of any debris such as leaves or branches or even a dead sheep. Generally, the water was delicious, and guests never complained of stomach upsets. However, it was occasionally known for a guest to find their bath full of brown water. Sometimes trippers or walkers would come in to the hotel and ask to fill up their water bottles. Rodney would politely tell them that the hotel got all its water from the beck and that they should do the same. Sometimes walkers would confidently stride through the hotel in search of a WC. Rodney's head would appear through the office window and he would sharply ask if he could help. They usually turned and fled.

The front cover of the 1959 hotel brochure

The summer of 1962 was appallingly wet. There were days of incessant rain and there was a great deal of flooding in the valley. To Rodney's alarm the swollen beck started to flow over the road, due to the heap of branches that had become lodged up against the bridge. The hotel ground floor was in danger of flooding and something had to be done urgently. When Rodney saw the problem, without hesitation he went into the beck in the pouring rain, with the surging water up to his chest, and one by one he threw the branches out on to the road. The staff

Inside the 1959 hotel brochure

BRIDGE HOTEL

●

The origin of the Hotel is rather obscure, but it was known as an inn in the early 19th century, variously called The Bridge Inn, and The Queen; it became The Victoria Hotel after a visit to Cumberland by the eldest daughter of Queen Victoria. On change of ownership in 1953 the name reverted to the " Bridge " once more, and a considerable number of structural alterations and improvements were made.

The Hotel is situated in one of Lakeland's most beautiful valleys. It is an ideal base for both the motorist and the fell walker. In addition, it is within easy access of many good rock climbs. Good fishing (trout, char and pike) is to be had in Buttermere and Crummock Water. National Trust rowing boats are available for hire on both lakes.

The house is well equipped throughout. There are two Lounges and a small Bar (conditional licence). All the 24 Bedrooms have fitted wash basins with running hot and cold water, bedside lamps and sockets for electric razors. There are 5 Bathrooms and 2 separate Showers. Partial central heating. Mains electricity throughout; electric fires available. Special Clothes-drying Room. Large Car Park.

Visitors are welcomed from Easter to the end of October, when the Hotel closes for the winter.

ACCESS

ROAD. There are three routes in from Keswick, i.e. Honister, Newlands and Whinlatter Passes. The first two have steep gradients (1 : 4) whilst the Whinlatter, which joins the road in from Cockermouth, is easy.

RAIL. The nearest station is Keswick. Taxis can be ordered without difficulty.

BUSES. There are daily services from Keswick and Cockermouth from the Spring Bank Holiday till mid-September. These services also run for a week at Easter. For the rest of the year there is a service from Cockermouth only, on Mondays and Saturdays.

and guests, from the comfort of the lounge and dining room windows, looked on with amazement and admiration as he struggled with an increasing tide of water flowing all around him. He most certainly saved the ground floor of the hotel from flooding, but unfortunately the cellar did not escape. A large number of wine bottles lost their labels and for some while Rodney would donate an unknown bottle of wine to the staff to drink with their dinner. Staff who were connoisseurs of wine sometimes had a very pleasant surprise.

Inside the 1959 hotel brochure

MEAL TIMES

Breakfast	8-45 a.m.
Lunch	1—2-0 p.m.
Tea	4-15 p.m.
Dinner	7-30 p.m.

Packed Lunches and Teas willingly provided.

●

TARIFF

En Pension—

£3 6 6 per day for stays of 2-6 days.

£20 10 0 per week (and *pro rata* for longer stays).

Our "en pension" terms include packed lunches and teas but we cannot make any reductions for meals not taken in the Hotel.

Lunch	13 6
Tea	4 6
Dinner	17 6

Dogs (welcome anywhere in the house, except the Dining-Room) ... 4/6 per day

●

BRIDGE HOTEL, BUTTERMERE, COCKERMOUTH,
CUMBERLAND

Proprietors: Telephone:
Mr. & Mrs. Rodney Twitchin   Buttermere 252

Resident Visitors' Telephone:
Buttermere 234

P.T.O.

While Rodney was troubleshooting, Rosemary, usually looking immaculate, was busy dealing with the correspondence, detailing work to the chambermaids, sorting the bed linen and creating beautiful flower arrangements for the lounges, the hall and the bar. She was an early convert to recycling and on her rounds of the bedrooms, after guests had left, she would collect up the partly used soaps and they would be used up by the family. Rosemary did not drive as fast as Rodney, but when she met another vehicle on one of the narrow lanes, she would not give way. Her tactic was to

The back cover of the 1959 hotel brochure

> ### GENERAL INFORMATION
>
> ●
>
> CHURCHES.   Church of England, Buttermere. Roman Catholic, Keswick and Cockermouth.
>
> We provide a good selection of newspapers and periodicals, and individual orders for newspapers can be arranged in advance.
>
> There are no shops in Buttermere. The nearest village shop is at Lorton (6 miles). We, however, keep a good selection of chocolate in the Hotel.
>
> We have our own Petrol Pump, but the nearest light repair facilities are 6 miles away.
>
> There is one postal delivery and collection a day, at 10-15 a.m. and 2 p.m. (Saturdays mid-day) respectively. Buttermere Post Office opens from 9 a.m.—3 p.m. Mondays to Fridays.
>
> Our electricity supply is 110 volts D.C. As the capacity of our plant is limited it would be appreciated if visitors did not bring travelling electric irons.
>
> Visitors are also requested not to bring detergents for any washing they may do, as these products damage our sewage system.
>
> Luggage in advance should be sent via Cockermouth.

continue at her same speed towards the vehicle so that the driver immediately panicked, went into reverse or rapidly pulled over to let Rosemary majestically swoop past.

Her pride and joy was her colourful garden at the back of the hotel. Here she spent many happy hours in seclusion tending her shrubs and flowers. There were many rose bushes and large clusters of hydrangeas were planted along the beck. On a summer's Sunday afternoon, she could be found weeding and listening with pleasure to 'Sing Something Simple', which was a programme of popular songs sung by the Cliff Adam Singers with an accordion accompaniment. Guests were not allowed to wander into her garden which had the notice 'Private' on the little white gate. Occasionally, however, a guest who claimed to be a keen gardener was given a guided tour. Rosemary had some casual help in the garden from an old boy called Dick Pringle (Rodney irreverently referred to him as Prick Dingle). He was short, his lack of height accentuated by stooping and he had a permanent dewdrop on the end of his nose. Like the lengthman, Syd Clark, he was one of the real old local characters.

No training was given to new student staff. They just had to ask the cook or the other waitresses what they had to do. As a result, the day to day work has been described by some as organised chaos but the atmosphere was always happy and relaxed. Rosemary with her Glynis Johns voice could be reproachful and was rather more feared than Rodney if things really did go wrong. Rodney was very rarely irritated by the staff but there were two things that did annoy him. One was when the staff persisted in hanging their laundry out on the balconies to dry. He did not like the guests to be greeted by rows of underwear when they arrived in the car park. The other thing that annoyed him was when staff innocently sat on the work surfaces in the kitchen. He would stop in front of the offender, stare fiercely, and say: 'Take the dirtiest part of your anatomy off that surface!' It did not happen again.

Once a waitress had a boyfriend living near the Cumbrian coast. One evening she clandestinely let him into the hotel, presumably for a night of passion. However, they were spotted embracing while saying goodbye in the car park the following morning. On hearing about this, Rodney was not too concerned about the morality of the visit, but he was very annoyed that the waitress and her young man had taken advantage of his hospitality without asking. If the young man had asked Rodney if he could stay the night, he might well have been told that he could, but that he should leave discretely before breakfast. After all, Rodney was always positively encouraging staff to get romantically involved with each other.

Rodney had a ribald sense of humour that was probably the result of being cooped up during the war for years in the desert with just his army chums. He often told the story how on one winter's day a particularly unattractive and unkempt woman came over from the Fish Hotel and asked Rodney for help with her census form. Rodney saw to his amusement that she had managed to fill in her name, address and age, but in the box for SEX she had innocently written 'twice a week'. Rodney had a fund of jokes and limericks. He enjoyed reciting the song about the three ladies who got locked in the lavatory and his favourite limericks were about the old lady from Bray and the young lady from Barking Creek. These unfortunate ladies all had their problems, but it was never the men, for some reason. I particularly remember one occasion when Rodney and I were closing the Bridge for the night. Rodney quietly beckoned me into the back lounge. I could hear a loud and regular creak emanating from the ceiling and it was rapidly becoming more urgent. Pointing upwards, Rodney gave me a wicked grin and whispered, 'That's Room 7 at it again!'

On the handyman's day off Rodney had to clean the guests' shoes. He always tried to lighten his load for the next day by promptly removing any guests' shoes that had put outside their rooms the evening before. This he felt would prevent other guests from realising that there was a shoe-cleaning service. After all, they could have their shoes cleaned by the handyman the following day. Rodney worked incredibly long and hard hours and he was constantly extremely tired so it is understandable that he wanted to lighten one of the duties of the handyman that he had to do on top of his already heavy schedule.

All the student staff were very fond of Rodney because he was extremely good-natured, He was always there to sort out any occasional misunderstandings or jealousies in a firm but kindly way. Rosemary was fairly cool in the way she managed the staff, but Rodney was always very supportive and aware if there was a problem. Carrie Watling, a young student in the early sixties, recalls that several staff had gone down with a nasty stomach bug. Carrie valiantly got up from her sick bed to offer much needed help, but Rodney seeing how ill she looked, promptly sent her back to bed. Such was his caring nature.

As he was frequently in the kitchen discussing the menus with the cook, Rodney regularly saw the kitchen staff and the waitresses. Every day, in order to get the wine that had been ordered for dinner, he would need to go down into the cellar which had a trap door in the floor of the tiny staff room. The staff were usually there hungrily eating their lunch. Then they had to remove their feet from the trap door and push back the table to allow Rodney to descend into the cellar. He would then emerge between the legs of the staff and laden with bottles. This was usually a time when Rodney could have a friendly chat to all the staff.

Rosemary did not have as much contact with the staff as Rodney, but she could be very talkative with the guests. However, if the conversation did not involve her, she would often have a long conversation with the dog instead, sometimes completely ignoring the fact that there was anyone else in the room. But when she wanted to, she could instantly bring out her warm personality accompanied by a beautiful smile. In the bar in the evenings she became more relaxed and she would sit, always behind the bar, putting her head to one side, listening intently to the conversation or the music.

By the end of October, it was time to close the hotel for the winter. Jen Hill worked and lived at the Bridge in the sixties for two years as the secretary and she continued to stay in the hotel during the winter months. She remembers that the first thing Rodney did was to catch up on his sleep. The day started at about 10 am with Rosemary dictating booking letters for the next season. They both did the Daily Telegraph crossword in the morning with Rodney often in his dressing gown. There was gardening to be done, the dog to be walked and laundry to be mended. In the evenings they would repair to the front lounge and play games or read. Life took on a leisurely pace. Every New Year's Day they opened up the Bridge and the well-stocked bar to friends and neighbours for a lunchtime drinks party, which was always a memorable occasion. Rodney and Rosemary had discovered the island of Gjerba, off the coast of Tunisia and for several years they would go there for a fortnight during the winter. Later on, they stayed with friends in the Caribbean.

Many friends and past staff were most welcome to come and stay for a few days while the hotel was closed. There was never any question of turning anyone away. There were always plenty of rooms available, of course. Rodney would do the cooking and there was a plentiful and varied supply of liquor from the bar. However, they never turned down the offer from visitors of a good meal in a hotel or restaurant and they always had plenty of local recommendations to offer. I remember while I was staying with them in the early sixties taking them to a hotel in Workington that was owned by the brewery. I impressed them greatly by buying a half bottle of 1955 Château d'Yquem, often described as the greatest dessert wine ever. It cost me an affordable £2, instead of over £100 today.

Rodney and Rosemary had little time to sit down and listen to music when the hotel was open. During the winter they particularly enjoyed listening to classical music and I remember Rodney telling me that one of his favourite pieces of music was Beethoven's 7th Symphony. In 1959 Sir Nicholas Secker opened the Rosehill Theatre near Whitehaven. The tiny auditorium's walls were lined with silk and it was once described as 'a rose-red silk lined jewel box'. The Twitchins fell in love with it and they attended concerts whenever they could. I was staying with them during the winter of

Carrie Watling on Prince with Zoë

1962 and we went to hear the world famous cellist, Paul Tortelier. We sat in the front row and it was a magical performance. Rodney treated these evenings as a formal occasion and he always wore his dinner jacket, although he was very much in the minority. When they retired, Rodney made a large collection of recordings of Mozart's concertos and symphonies. Rosemary attended art classes; she particularly enjoyed painting watercolours of flowers.

During the holidays Rollo and Zoë would return from school. Zoë boarded at St Anne's school in Windermere and Rollo went to St Bees school near Whitehaven. Zoë had her pony, Prince which kept her busy for several years and Rollo had his bicycle.

He could be seen in the village dashing up and down the steep and winding road or riding over a homemade obstacle course when he occasionally suffered a nasty spill. He took an interest in the farms and later in the hotel. He went through a phase of being a bit cheeky with the staff, as boys will, but Rodney swiftly put a stop to that. The guests were always pleased to see Rollo and Zoë, and they both added a happy family atmosphere to the hotel.

In the new year the hotel was always bustling with workmen. The hotel was never enlarged or the rooms reorganised, but there was a continuous programme of replacing plumbing, rewiring and generally sprucing up the bedrooms with redecoration and laying new linoleum in the bathrooms. The kitchen had to be deep cleaned and the whole hotel had to have a thorough spring clean. Charlie Bateman was the local builder and Rodney was popular with his workforce because they were always given a pint of beer at lunchtime. Then there were dozens of curtains and covers to be cleaned and they all had to be hung up or returned to their original place before the hotel opened. And so Easter came around again with the same loyal daily staff, new students and the hope of a good summer and a full hotel.

5

It Takes All Sorts

The new hotel proprietors wanted their guests to be interesting, well-spoken and from the middle classes; indeed, people who they thought would enjoy their type of hospitality. In addition, they were looking for those who were country lovers and keen on walking, who would fall in love with the Lakes and would really want to return. They hated coaches or charabancs as Rodney called them and they thought, perhaps unfairly, that day trippers were bad for the Lakes. Rodney refused to have a vacancy sign outside the hotel, possibly thinking back to the days when his mother ran a rather less exclusive guest house.

In the early years they were desperate to fill the hotel, yet if they did not like the accent of someone who rang up to book a room, they would say that the hotel was full. Around this time a young secretary turned a couple away who she thought were unsuitable guests. Two of the kitchen staff overheard this and knowing that the hotel was not full, complained to Rodney about the secretary's biased behaviour. As usual Rodney defused the situation without censoring the secretary. All this may sound very snobbish and non-politically correct today, but this selection process, together with Rodney and Rosemary's warm personalities, created a hotel that was soon full of guests who got on well together and wanted to return time and time again.

I have looked at the visitors' books for the Easter weekends from 1954 through to Easter 1969. They show that their first Easter in 1954 had 21 out of 24 rooms booked over the holiday weekend with 31 guests out of a possible 38. For their first Easter I think that this must have been a very encouraging number of guests: however, after the holiday break the numbers fell dramatically. Easter 1955 was almost full again but with only one guest who had stayed the Easter before. In Easter 1956 the hotel was full and from then on Easter became the most popular time for guests. By Easter 1960 at least half the hotel was filled with guests that had stayed the previous Easter.

So, Easter at the Bridge became an occasion to meet up with old friends and acquaintances. Many guests returned year after year, three couples staying at Easter at least ten times. The regulars always bagged the more spacious bedrooms at the front of the hotel. The most frequent were Stephen and Gwen Harbottle (he was a solicitor from Gosforth) who always stayed in Room 4, Mr Lovelock who was headmaster of Lime House Preparatory School in Dalston in Cumberland and Dennis and Ness Weaver who were known to be keen walkers and liked Room 3. Mr and Mrs Littlewood

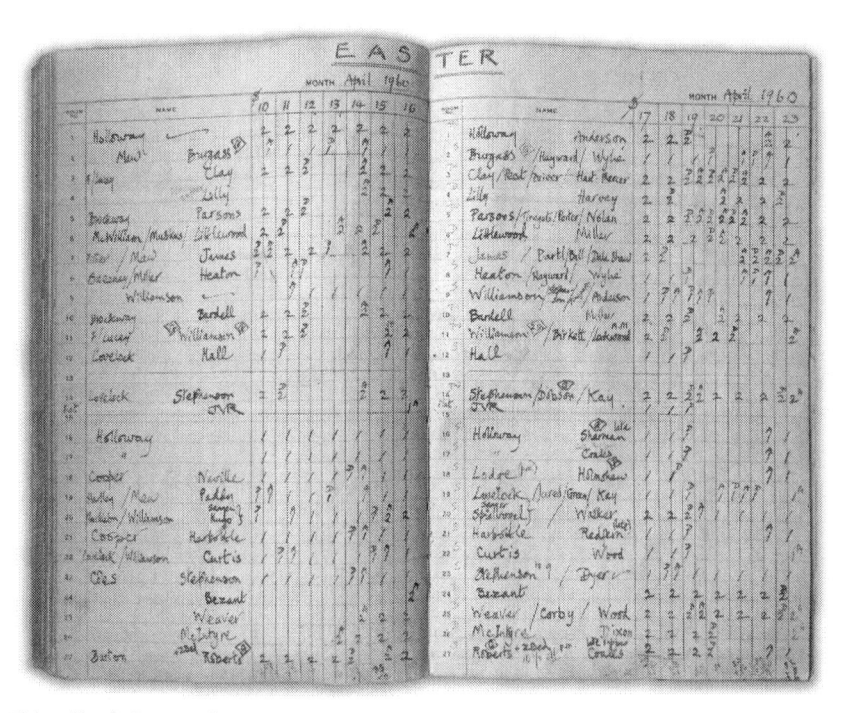

Visitors' book, Easter 1960

stayed nine times and Mr and Mrs Parsons from Dundee (who stayed in Room 1) stayed eight times.

Perhaps the most regular Easter guest was young Neville Lodge. He stayed for the first and second Easter and stayed in the hotel at least eighteen times. He would always have the single Room 18. His family had a successful clothing firm in Leeds and as a result he owned a very snazzy Bristol AC car which greatly impressed the female staff. I was impressed with the car as well and I remember before the days of a blanket 70 mph speed limit, Neville driving me to Cockermouth and on returning reaching over 100 mph on the straight, just slowing down in time for the inevitable bends. Wow!

The Bridge's good reputation was beginning to be passed on by the guests and an example of this was when two rather eccentric and extremely academic gentlemen stayed there in August 1953. One was the educationist Frederick Happold (who wrote a book about mysticism) and the other, his classicist friend Dr Arthur Peck (who translated Aristotle into English from the Greek). Dr Peck was an old friend of my family in Cambridge and he returned from the Lakes to strongly recommend the Bridge to my parents. They were suitably impressed and my family soon stayed there. We made several visits as a family and it was not long before a lasting friendship with the Twitchins was made between us. While a student I was the handyman for part of my holidays in 1958 and 1959. Afterwards I returned many times as a paying guest. Like several other handymen, such was the lure of the Bridge that I spent part of my honeymoon there in 1965, as well as many other visits to stay with the Twitchins during the winter.

A notable regular at Easter was Elsie Burgass, whose husband had served with Rodney in the army during the war. She always stayed in Room 2 and, perhaps because she was a friend of Rodney's, she was particularly demanding on the staff. She continually smoked small cigars, made liberal use of the perfume bottle and she always had the heating in her room on maximum. The result was that if you entered her room you were met with a wall of hot, heavily scented smoke that almost knocked you backwards. The chambermaids who made up the room complained of feeling quite nauseous during their duties. Elsie was known to fall off her bar stool in the evenings but of course this was put down to her poor sense of balance.

Ex-handyman, Tim Cartmell, recalls that when he was filling Elsie's car with petrol, he pointed out to her that the choke handle on her rusty old Triumph Herald was pulled out. She explained that it was an extremely useful handle for her handbag and when she was driving this was where her handbag was always hung. The car appeared to have behaved perfectly well all the way from south of London despite this abuse. Elsie kept a collapsible boat at Wood House and she spent many happy days in it fishing on Crummock Water.

An unmarried couple in their thirties whose surnames began with H and C were regulars at Easter, so Rodney immediately christened them Hot and Cold. Rodney was certainly not a prude, but if a couple arrived who were not married he would rather mischievously make sure they were in bedrooms on a different floor. He applied this rule to Hot and Cold and he though it must have been effective when a guest reported that he had nearly tripped over the pair being very busy lying in the bracken. He commented that he thought it was high time they got married. Alas, it was rumoured that the couple's parents had already forbidden them to be married and that ban must have lasted for at least the eight Easters that they stayed at the Bridge in single rooms. Curiously they never signed the visitors' book.

Jo Jared became a regular guest. He was a ship's engineer on the Ellerman Line and sailed in the SS *Palmelian*. This was a cargo steamer of 1,500 tons which was launched in 1947 and scrapped in 1970. The first time Jo arrived at the Bridge he rang the office bell for attention. The glass window slid open with a crash and Rodney's rather stern mother, who was staying at the time, shoved her head through the gap and abruptly demanded if she could be of any help. Jo meant to explain that as he was a ship's engineer, he could be called away suddenly at any time, and this would shorten his intended stay. Instead of this, somewhat flummoxed by his formidable reception, he spluttered 'I'm a sea-faring man'. Before he could say any more, Rodney and Rosemary, who were in the office and must have overheard the conversation, appeared from around the corner. Side by side, with their arms folded and giggling uncontrollably, they proceeded to dance the hornpipe; to the amusement of Jo and the astonishment of Rodney's mother. No wonder that from then on Jo always referred to the Bridge as the lunatic asylum.

Jo was always very generous when staff were in the bar and he encouraged them to order a Rod Collins on him. This was a cocktail of gin, ginger beer and Angostura bitters. However, this drink was not popular with Rodney as the rims of the glasses had to be coated with egg white and sugar. Later in the evening this gave Rodney some difficulty with the washing up. Being a sea-faring man, Jo was particularly partial to a pink gin. Late one evening he was negotiating the back stairs and fell. Cursing, he tumbled down head first, shot across the passageway and hit his head with a crash on the lounge wall. He knocked himself out but miraculously by the next day his head had recovered. The wall, however, was left with a large hole in the plasterboard, which must have been a talking point with both the other guests and the staff. Jo invented the incredibly challenging route called the Buttermere and Crummock Round and this is described in a later chapter.

Another regular guest was Gwilym Morgan, an Anglican priest from Lancashire and who became a Canon in 1962. A bachelor, he had a wicked sense of humour and one day he asked Zoë if he could ride her pony called Prince. Of course, the weather was wet and so Prince's feet were muddy. However, this did not stop Gwilym, looking rather large on a very small pony, riding up to the front door of the hotel and through the hall to the office window. Gwilym then leant over Prince's neck and rang the bell. Rodney opened the frosted window to be confronted by the pony's head and Gwilym's torso. Rodney could see that Prince had left a trail of dirty hoof marks across the hall carpet and he quite reasonably made some acerbic remark. In response to Rodney's negative reaction to his visit, Prince lifted his tail in the hall and proceeded to make matters worse.

Early visitors to the Bridge were the Hill family. Joselyn was a solicitor in London and he would arrive en masse with his wife Bunny, his four daughters and two grandparents. The daughters amusingly had the initials R, S, V and P; other than Rowan, I have not been able to discover their first names. The daughters were all keen on painting and consequently they made frequent visits to the kitchen for water. Tim Cartmell, who was a handyman three times in the sixties, got to know the Hills very well and he was eventually articled to Joselyn's firm of solicitors.

Jaap van Rees, a Dutchman as his name implies, first visited the Bridge in 1958. He was living in Morecambe and working as a civil engineer for the firm Harbour and General. He was lonely and he had been told by a friend that he should find a holiday location where he would be really happy and would want to return regularly. In this way the owners and staff would get to know him and remember all his likes and dislikes. Jaap chose the Bridge and he immediately enjoyed the warm friendly atmosphere of the hotel. It was not long before he was a regular guest at weekends. He became good friends of the Twitchins and, being the Bridge, if he requested a room there was always a bed available for him. If no guest room was available, he was happy to be given a staff room instead. In order to prolong his stay, he would leave early for work on the Monday morning having breakfasted with the staff. He later wrote in his autobiography that these journeys home at half past seven in the morning driving over Newlands Pass, were when he saw the Lakes at their most beautiful.

Jaap got on particularly well with Rodney and there were often discussions about the opposite sex. As we know, Rodney was particularly keen on encouraging young staff to have romantic interests and he noticed that a student nurse working as a waitress might just be the right match for Jaap. Jaap's birthday was in May and in 1960 he was very surprised to get a birthday card signed by Rodney and Rosemary as well as a few of the living-in staff. It had a drawing of a harassed nurse with the words '<u>DO</u> GET WELL SOON'. However, the word WELL had been changed to WED. Rodney had written on the back:

'The reason for this rather "odd" card is that we have no proper birthday ones in stock.

The emphasis on the nursing profession is to advise you that we have a 23 year old 'peach' (name Tilly) working for us. Worth looking at, deadly efficient, good sense of humour and, we think, might appeal to you. She won't be on view on Saturday or Sunday morning as she has a boy-friend coming to see her!! If I were single, I wouldn't hesitate a second!!'

The following weekend Jaap stayed at the Bridge and he was delighted to find Tilly waiting on him at dinner. He carefully chose a bottle of claret called Saint Amour to drink with his meal, hoping that Tilly would take the hint. They must have met in the bar later that evening for some social drinking, when they would have got to know each other better. The next day Tilly had to get to her parents' home which was over 50 miles away in Ravenstonedale, near Kirkby Stephen. Jaap, seizing the opportunity, offered to give her a lift home. Tilly's parents obviously approved of Jaap, as they invited him to stay the night and only four months later Tilly and Jaap were married. This was one of several marriages that resulted from meetings at the Bridge.

Hugo Spielvogel was a middle-aged East European who lived in Doncaster. He stayed at least 16 times at the Bridge and his favourite time was Easter. He particularly enjoyed his food and the wine at dinner. He never did any serious walking, which you could tell from his generous figure, and if he did venture on to the fells he was soon complaining of 'puffingstopitis'. He had a daily order for sour cream, which may have been to settle his stomach from the previous evening. It was provided by Ann and Mike Kyle at Syke Farm, and they insisted on not charging for this. However, Hugo would put some money for the Kyles in an envelope and give it to Irene Gibson at the end of his stay. His cure for a hangover was raw eggs, and not surprisingly, he did not manage to persuade anyone else to use this remedy. Hugo was always extremely generous in the bar and I remember that this could sometimes cause him some embarrassment when he received his hotel bill.

Rodney and Rosemary would do the Daily Telegraph crossword in the bar in the evenings when they were not busy serving. On one occasion when Hugo Spielvogel and Jaap van Rees were in the bar, Rodney handed them the uncompleted crossword, asking if they could help with a clue. Within minutes they had finished the whole crossword and Hugo exclaimed, 'It takes two bloody foreigners to complete the Daily Telegraph crossword!'. His remark caused a lot of laughter among those present.

Alfred Wainwright (1907-1991) was famous for his pictorial guides to the Lake District. While he was researching his guide to the Western Fells in 1947, he stayed in Room 1. Before he died, he asked that his ashes should be scattered 'on his favourite spot on earth', by the side of the Innominate Tarn on Haystacks. There is a commemorative window to him in Buttermere church that very fittingly looks out towards Haystacks.

There were not many distinguished guests: perhaps the style of management was not serious or professional enough for them. However, two guests are worth mentioning. One was the Labour MP Philip Noel-Baker, who was the only person to win an Olympic medal as well as the Nobel Prize. He was made a Life Peer in 1977. The other was the physicist Lord Adrian, who was President of the Royal Society and also a Nobel Prize winner. He was ennobled in 1955.

A small boost to the guest numbers was the result of the Seascale Riding School bringing up to 12 riders to stay at the Bridge for a night on 13 occasions in 1954 and 1955. While the guests no doubt enjoyed the comforts of the hotel, the horses or ponies were given grazing in the Twitchins' paddock across the road.

Guests were not encouraged to bring babies or very small children and as a result the hotel had a rather peaceful and genteel atmosphere. Indeed, there were no facilities for children at all. There was no games room with darts, pool or a table tennis table. There were no lawns where children could let off steam by playing cricket or football. The lounges, according to one handyman, had a funereal atmosphere about them, which must have meant that any children were told to pipe down. Clearly children were expected to dutifully accompany their parents on long boring walks over the sodden fells, or on a very wet day be taken to visit the pencil factory in Keswick, which in my youth I found particularly boring.

Dogs were allowed and they could sleep in the bedrooms. There was a modest charge of 2/6d per day in 1959. A few dogs unfortunately misbehaved during their stay and Rodney took exception to these accidents. In his mischievous way he would later put a plastic dog poop on the carpet in the dog owner's room, in the hope that its discovery would give the owner a temporary distasteful shock. No doubt a member of staff had already had an unpleasant experience making the discovery and this was Rodney's way of quietly getting his own back. All the staff knew what Rodney had done.

Not only did dogs misbehave but in the Twitchins' view some guests could as well. Good social graces were expected. It might be that guests left their rooms in disarray, making the chambermaids job difficult. Guests who were continually late for meals also brought disapproval, particularly from the cook. Jo Jared was always late for breakfast, but somehow, he managed to avoid any criticism from Rodney or the staff. A few guests who were rude to the staff or generally difficult were not tolerated at all and Rodney would try to make them so uncomfortable that they did not wish to stay again. The commercial consequences did not matter: standards had to be maintained! Handyman, John Scadding, remembers meeting a professional pianist in the hotel and together they played a duet on the piano in the back lounge one afternoon when the hotel seemed empty of guests. Soon there was the loud thumping noise of a walking stick from a room above. Obviously, a guest had been disturbed and they instantly stopped playing. John then mentioned this to Rodney, who immediately suggested that they should continue playing, as he was not fond of the guest!

There was a Mr White who let the bath water overflow which caused considerable damage to a ceiling and to the furnishings in the room below. Rodney could be quite irritated by such antisocial behaviour and he would have discussed this at some length with the staff who had to clear up the mess. From then on Rodney referred to the miscreant as 'Bath Water White'.

Guests were encouraged by the Twitchins to go out on to the fells whatever the weather. This exodus helped to free the bedrooms for the chambermaids and it kept the lounges more available for cleaning.

Rodney also encouraged the more agile guests and the student staff to race up the neighbouring peaks and to discuss the times taken in the bar later in order to find out if records had been broken. On Easter Mondays guests were expected to walk up to Haystacks where there was a disorganised game of Hare and Hounds.

Rodney could be rather disparaging about any guests that he felt did not fit in with the ethos of the hotel. He would readily share his thoughts with the staff, who would usually agree with his sentiments, and he would play a rather cheeky little joke. A liqueur bottle behind the bar had a stopper topped with a wooden elephant. This had an articulated tail. Normally the tail would be proudly erect, but while an unpopular guest was staying Rodney would move the tail to a forlorn downward

Rodney and Rosemary in the bar with the elephant's tail down

position. All the staff and some favoured guests would know who the unpopular guest was and when that guest arrived and departed.

Because of the unique style of management, many guests became good acquaintances and often lifelong friends of Rodney and Rosemary. For the average guest, having settled the hotel bill, there would be a handshake through the office window and the handyman would then carry the suitcases to the car. For more favoured guests, Rodney and Rosemary would go outside with the guests and wave to them as they drove away. And for those who were good friends, the whole Twitchin family would accompany the guests to their car and bid farewell with warm embraces.

6

Food, Glorious Food

Good food was almost non-existent in pubs in the fifties and very few hotels were providing gourmet meals. In family-run hotels there was not a high expectation for fine food and as long as it was plentiful, wholesome and suitably hot, it would do. Rodney wanted to give guests excellent food and so when he took over the Bridge, he employed Elizabeth Audland, who had been Cordon Bleu trained. The food she produced was certainly good, but she had to contend with an old-fashioned kitchen and a budget which did not allow for expensive ingredients. So, the meals were not very exciting, and the main courses were rather plain by today's standards. Many of the guests were keen walkers and certainly enough wholesome food must have been presented each day to satisfy their appetites. As there were few complaints about the food it also must have been good.

The kitchen was always extremely busy as there were so many meals to prepare every day. Guests could have early morning tea from 7 am; and even breakfast in bed. The staff had their breakfast in the cramped staff room before the guests had theirs. The Twitchins had their meals in the office. Breakfast in the dining room was from 8.45 am, which some guests thought was too late if they wanted to go for a serious long walk on the fells. There was the traditional half grapefruit or orange juice, cereals and a cooked English breakfast. At breakfast or lunch guests had to choose and order their wine for dinner that evening, because Rodney simply had too much to do in the evenings and he could then get the wine from the cellar well in advance. Walkers could order a substantial packed lunch which included sandwiches, fruit loaf and fruit. Then there were the walkers' thermoses to be filled with tea or coffee. After all that, it was not long before residents and chance visitors would be ordering coffee in the front lounge or the dining room.

Most guests went out for the day to walk in the fells, and unless the weather was very wet, only a few guests stayed in the hotel for lunch. This meant that there was plenty of room in the dining room for a regular stream of non-walking visitors who enjoyed a three-course meal with a choice for the main course and tea or coffee to follow. In 1959 lunch cost 7/6d. Rodney always felt that this was profitable extra income and he got quite excited on bank holidays when there was the need for two lunch sittings. He manned the bar at lunchtime, sometimes with Rosemary's help, and served the drinks to the diners. The staff had their lunch as soon as the dining room was empty.

Tea for residents was served in the back lounge at 4 pm and non-residents were served in the dining room. In the back lounge tea was laid out on a table and you helped yourself. There were scones with jam, cream and the local delicacy, homemade rum butter. There were orange and lemon sponge cakes as well as homemade fruit cake. Sedentary guests who had already had a cooked breakfast, a large lunch and then had tea, were in danger of spoiling their appetites for dinner. But no one counted calories in those days.

Before dinner the Twitchins would open up the bar for pre-dinner drinks. Rosemary would drink her Croft Original sherry and light a cigarette. She was a light smoker, but Rodney was seldom seen without a Player's Navy Cut cigarette.

Dinner was heralded by a Burmese brass gong in the hall that was vigorously struck by the cook at precisely 7.30 pm. The dining room could seat forty people and the tables were square with white linen table cloths. The guests had their own linen napkins for the length of their stay, which remained on their table in red envelopes with their names or room numbers on them. Two waitresses would be on duty wearing maroon dresses with a white apron and they would ask the guests if they wanted soup or melon. Once a waitress came back into the kitchen laughing her head off because she had asked a table if they wanted 'moup or selon', to the guests' amusement. These were always the starters and they were hardly very imaginative.

There was no choice for the main course at dinner, but it was always mainstream such as chicken, veal, beef or pork. If Syd Clark had visited, then the guests would be treated to salmon. Vegetables were very predictable and served in white oval dishes with, for example, mashed potato at one end and cauliflower at the other. On Fridays it was fish and on Sundays

```
           Menu  22.8.58.

              L U N C H
              ─────────

            Fruit Juice
                OR
            "Bridge" Soup
                ***

     Baked Cod, Shrimp Sauce,
             Spring Cabbage,
                OR
     Gilled Pork Chops, Apple Sauce,
             Spring Cabbage,
                OR
        Cold Veal and Ham Pie,
                Salad,
            New  Potatoes
                ***

     Steamed Orange Pudding and
                    Orange Sauce,
                OR
        Cheese and Biscuits
                ***

            Tea or Coffee
                ***
```

The Bridge Hotel lunch menu from 1958

there was no cook, so the waitresses had great fun making French onion soup and usually a cold collation was served up for the main course. There were always simple desserts such as pink blancmange or fruit salad, followed by the varied cheeseboard. After dinner coffee was always put in the hall to be drunk in either of the two lounges.

Rodney was able to buy some excellent wines at very reasonable prices from the Workington brewery. The brewery obviously knew their wines and consequently the Bridge had a fine wine list. In the fifties, at the cheapest end of the wine list I well remember that there was a red Cobières Superior from the Languedoc and a white Entre-deux-Mers from Bordeaux. They sold for 8/- a bottle or 5/- a half bottle. At the other end of the scale, if you really wanted to push the boat out, there were several fine wines, such as a buttery white Meursault from Burgundy or a rich red Château Pichon-Longueville from Bordeaux. To the wine connoisseur's delight, both of these were priced in the fifties at under £2 a bottle. Wine was never served by the glass and often guests did not finish their bottle of wine. These bottles were marked with their room numbers and lined up on the sideboard to be used the next day. Because everyone sat down at the same time Rodney had a very difficult time getting all the wine served with the main course and he sometimes told the waitresses to slow down the serving to give him extra time. If the hotel was full, this was a stressful time for Rodney, and he did not appreciate the guests who ordered their wines at the last minute.

The guests probably did not realise that the staff could only eat their evening meal once the dining room was empty. Guests who lingered in deep conversation over the cheese course were not popular. By the time the tables had been cleared and laid for breakfast, the staff were ravenous. Frequently they did not sit down to eat until 10 pm or later. The food was usually the same as served to the guests, so the staff felt that they were being well fed. Rodney would donate a bottle or two of wine to the staff if he felt that the day had been successful and that everyone had worked hard.

The atmosphere in the kitchen was particularly hectic before and during dinner and sometimes it could be chaotic. The cook reigned and latecomers for dinner were the cause of many of her tantrums. Rodney liked a few formalities and he never wanted the cook to be called by her first name. Consequently, she was known as 'Cookie' by the staff. Woe betide the handyman who failed to riddle the Aga sufficiently or forgot to fill it up with coke. If the Aga went out it was a major calamity as there was so little other equipment in the kitchen on which to cook up to forty meals. Then Cookie would be down on the handyman like a ton of bricks. After so many cooks and handymen had struggled with the temperamental Aga for years, Rodney eventually installed a commercial gas cooker with four ovens that ran on LPG.

Dorothy Fell was a very popular young cook who arrived from Kendal on her scooter to start her new job. She followed Elizabeth Audland and she got on extremely well with the student staff. They were always joking together and playing tricks on each other. One year, just after the hotel had opened for the season, Dorothy put her head round the office door and said, 'There's a lamb in my oven.' Rodney and Rosemary were somewhat surprised as lamb was definitely not on the menu that evening and so they questioned her further. Dorothy repeated what she had said and after waiting for Rodney and Rosemary to be completely puzzled, she explained that the neighbouring farmer, Robbie Jackson, had called in holding a new-born lamb. The lamb was orphaned and rather sickly, so he wanted it to be put in a warm environment. The Aga in the Bridge's kitchen seemed to be the perfect spot and so Dorothy had let him tenderly place the lamb in the slow oven; with the door open. Of course. Rodney and Rosemary then saw the funny side of it and rushed into the kitchen to have a good look at their extra guest.

Dorothy and a 'poached' salmon

The groceries were ordered from Giff Bewcher in Cockermouth who made a daily delivery and the poultry came from the Richardson farmers in Seathwaite. Two gallons of fresh milk were delivered daily, first from the Gibsons and then later on from Mike Kyle's Ayrshire cows at Syke Farm. Occasionally the Bridge would run out of milk and someone would be sent round to collect more, sometimes as late as 10 pm. This was never a problem to the Kyles, who were always helpful neighbours. Charlie Bateman, the local builder, had friends who were fishermen and so he regularly supplied the Bridge with freshly caught fish. The cook chose the food for the menus and Rodney always checked it for quality. Rodney rarely interfered with the cook's choice of menus, but having spent some years in Rangoon, he did insist that rice pudding should never be served to the guests. In his view rice should only be used as a vegetable.

There was a large indispensable commercial dishwasher in the scullery (known as the still-room). One very busy August bank holiday, when Buttermere was sweltering in a heatwave, the dishwasher broke down and flooded the still-room and part of the kitchen. Rodney was urgently called up on the intercom that connected the kitchen and the office. This was a disaster at a time when guests were waiting to be served in the dining room, but everybody kept calm and with Rodney's help the water was all mopped up. It was a trying situation for the staff who were working in tropical conditions. Typically, no one became ill-tempered and everyone worked together to clear up the mess, and later there were free drinks all round for those who had helped.

Another emergency was when Sheila, a later cook, carelessly cut off the top of her thumb with the meat slicer. After a frantic search by the cook and the kitchen staff, the bloody and rather dirty tip was found on the floor. Jen Hill, the secretary, drove the rather subdued and tearful Sheila, holding her bandaged thumb and its severed tip, to Keswick cottage hospital. Hoping that the tip could swiftly be reunited with its thumb Jen found a nurse who she knew well and desperately asked her if a minor operation could immediately be performed to sew the tip back on to the thumb. The nurse took one look at the thumb tip, and to Sheila and Jen's horror, immediately threw it into a bin.

Turning to Jen she said, 'Ee, bloody 'ell, Miss Jennifer, this is nowt good t'anyone.'

So sadly, they had to return without the tip, and presumably the thumb healed over in due course. There was no Health and Safety Executive in those days and as far as I know, no Safety Book either in which to log the accident.

Irene was the assistant cook and she took her job seriously. There were several kitchen staff that she had to manage and keep an eye on. One of her jobs at the start of the season was to make fifty fruit loaves wrapped up in foil for future packed lunches and teas, and these were supposed to last the summer. One day she noticed that after several of the loaves had been sliced up, some of the slices were disappearing. So she kept a weather eye open and she caught a chubby waitress helping herself to the slices of loaf. When Irene challenged her, she replied that she was just checking the number of slices.

'No,' said Irene, 'I saw you eating some and this is not the first time you have done it. If I ever catch you doing this again you will be out on your ear.'

The student retorted, 'You can't do that. Only Rodney can sack me.'

'Oh, yes I can,' said Irene, 'And anyway you need to slim.'

'Are you calling me fat?' she responded.

'No,' said Irene, 'But you definitely need to slim.'

There was no more stealing after that. Irene told me this story with glee in 2018, when she was ninety years old.

Generally, the cooks gave their notice amicably for whatever reason and left at the end of the season. However, one day Rodney got so fed up with a cook who regularly over-ordered the groceries and produced such mediocre meals that, very unusually for Rodney, he flew into a rage and sacked her on the spot. He told her to pack her bags and to leave immediately. That afternoon Ollie Maurice, the handyman, was asked to drive (he thought rather unfairly) the weeping and wailing cook to Keswick station. Feeling somewhat disgruntled, he returned to the Bridge and he was then dismayed to be asked if he would cook dinner that evening for thirty-six guests. The Twitchins must have been going out for the evening, or Rodney would have stepped into the breach. At the young age of twenty-three, with no cooking experience, Ollie was suddenly propelled into becoming the hotel cook for the evening. Zoë, then a young teenager, was very keen to assist and between them they produced lemon soup, boeuf bourguignon and mousse au chocolat Basque. The guests must have felt that the result was a triumph, as they celebrated it by washing the food down with a few bottles of the best Burgundy wines on offer, which were Meursault and Beaune. The dinner was declared by everyone to have been a great success.

Photograph Album

1. *Rodney with Rollo, Zoë and Brandy*

2. Rodney

3. Dorothy and friend with the hotel behind them

4. In the Kitchen. Pomme, Dorothy and Odilia

5. Odilia's 21st birthday. Left to right: Zetta, Pomme, Sybil, Irene, Dorothy and Lizzie with Odilia in front

6. Local friends of the Twitchins often visited the bar

7. *Sketch of Pomme by Zetta*

8. Rodney returning from serving petrol in the rain

9. Sybil and Dorothy

10. Sheila, Jane, Vanessa and Brandy – tea in the sunshine

11. *The Austin Seven – beside Loweswater. Lizzie, a chambermaid, declared 'It's nowt but a lal biscuit tin'. It was my means of transport in 1959.*

7

Fun and Games

The bar was a small room at the rear of the hotel. It was furnished with a gleaming hardwood bar top which Rodney lovingly polished each day, some fine three-legged bar stools made by the local joiner Charlie Bateman and benches with cushions placed along the walls. It had an intimate atmosphere with its plates on the wall behind the bar, as well as pictures of the Lake District around the room and photographs of the owners' dogs past and present. There were always fresh flowers that had been carefully arranged by Rosemary and had been picked by her from her garden. She would sit elegantly on a stool behind the bar, with the porthole behind her through which she could periodically glance. This meant that she could see anyone entering or leaving the hotel by the front door, which was a good security arrangement. Often in the evening the bar would be very crowded with a thick haze of cigar, pipe and cigarette smoke that did not seem to bother anybody. No snacks were available in the bar, which as it was often heaving, was probably just as well.

There was one draught beer available, which was the excellent Workington Golden Bitter, and cider was available on draught. My sister, Alison Steer who worked at the Bridge from 1962-64, remembers drinking cider out of a Victorian triple-handled pewter three-pint mug. Many years later it was engraved with the names John, Thea and Alison, which were my parents' and my sister's names. There was also bottled beer such as Double Diamond and Newcastle Brown. Spirits were a few brands each of brandy, gin, rum, vodka and whisky. There was Angostura Bitters for pink gins, which were drunk by nautical guests. Also, a small bottle of Fernet-Branca, a bitter herbal liqueur that was good apparently for flatulence as well as hangovers. This came in handy for guests and staff after many a night in the bar. Then there were the time-honoured aperitifs such as Campari, Cinzano and Pernod.

There was also a large range of liqueurs – Drambuie, Crème de Menthe, Cointreau, Grand Marnier, Green and Yellow Chartreuse – to name a few. Probably more than a dozen. One night when I was a handyman, having had several drinks already, I was persuaded to buy one measure of each liqueur. I think it was my birthday. I certainly did not like all of those concoctions, but the sickly experiment did not give me any ill effects.

A tradition at the Bridge was to give guests the 'barmaid's drip'. If a group of guests were drinking spirits, they were wise to watch the level of the upturned bottles with their optics. If the level in a bottle was very low and the guest could gauge that there was less that two full optics of a spirit remaining in the bottle, he would quickly ask for a measure. A full optic would be dispensed and if the optic did not then fill up completely, the final 'drip' was added to the glass free of charge. I have never seen this generous act in any other hostelry.

The Twitchins also gave an inscribed half-pint pewter tankard to the first 20 guests who had stayed at the Bridge ten times (I was given one, although with typical generosity Rodney and Rosemary allowed my turns as a handyman to be counted, as well as my stays as a guest). These mugs hung in the bar until the hotel was sold and then the mugs were given to the respective guests. Each mug had an engraving that Rodney had devised, and the designs were jokingly connected to the recipient's character. One ex-handyman, who became a regular guest, had a ram's head on his mug and another guest, a pair of underpants. Discretion does not allow the reasons for these designs to be divulged. Another guest, a doctor called Chercowski, had a rebus on his mug which depicted a cow sitting on a chair with a ski leaning against it.

FUN AND GAMES

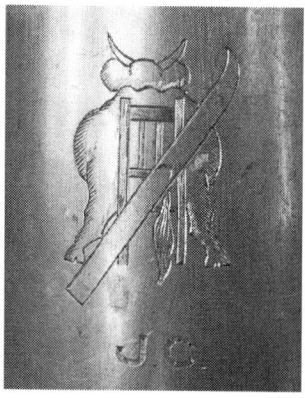

Chercowski's mug, engraved with a cow sitting on a chair with a ski

The Director of the Workington brewery, Tim Iredale, regularly visited the Bridge to discuss Rodney's requirements for the bar and the dining room. Tim wore a wooden leg, and everyone could always tell when he was visiting because his leg squeaked ominously when he walked and anyone who met him had to keep a straight face.

Rodney would man the bar late into the evenings, holding a tankard of bitter. If he was asked by one of the guests if he would like a drink, he would draw an inch of bitter into his tankard and charge the guest accordingly. He was thus not only very considerate but, in the main, sober as well. Rosemary also served in the bar if it was busy, and having a sweet tooth, she would drink her medium sherry before dinner and later, perhaps, just one liqueur. In front of where she sat there were several small pieces of paper on a shelf, on which there were quotations or little poems to amuse her when the conversation got a bit boring. One of these was a delightful Irish ditty, which sounded pretty idyllic.

I always enjoyed reading this when I occasionally served behind the bar. It was easy to remember.

> *Oh, that the peat would cut itself*
> *And the fish would leap ashore.*
> *Then you and I could lie abed*
> *And love for evermore.*

The hotel had a conditional licence which meant that only guests who were eating a meal or staying in the hotel could be served alcoholic drinks. The Fish Hotel, a hundred yards away, catered for all those visitors to Buttermere who were not staying or eating at the Bridge. The Twitchins liked to think that the Bridge was superior to the Fish, while at the same time they were envious of its public bar takings. However, many guests and staff have said that the conditional licence meant that the exclusiveness of the bar at the Bridge gave it a wonderfully intimate and friendly atmosphere. Despite the restriction of a conditional licence, occasionally Rodney would furtively invite a few local friends into the bar, and they would really enliven the evening, giving it an extra dimension by passing on the local gossip.

Unusually for a hotel the resident student staff were always welcome in the bar after dinner. Indeed, handymen were asked to run the bar on the few occasions that Rodney and Rosemary were out during the evening. Allowing staff to drink in the bar was good for bar takings and students have always been hearty drinkers. Another reason for the popularity of the bar was that there was absolutely no television reception in Buttermere. Having no televisions or telephones in all the hotel rooms might have deterred the more demanding guests, but the Twitchins were not seeking that sort of clientele.

The first cook, Elizabeth Audland, kept a highland pony called Muffet. Some warm summer evenings after she had been out riding, Elizabeth would stop outside the door into the back of the bar and Muffet would put her head inside. Rodney would delightedly produce a frothing bucket of Workington Best Bitter and with several noisy slurps and snorts, Muffet would empty it. This never ceased to amuse anyone who was in the bar at the time.

Singing in the bar was a frequent occurrence and a favourite rendition was four-part harmony singing. The tune was from one of the psalms and the words were taken from a description of the hotel in the brochure. This was started in the late sixties by Robert Ponsonby who was a good friend of the Twitchins. The handyman, John Scadding, remembers singing the bass line, Zoë singing soprano and Robert as tenor. At weekends or when there was an anniversary to celebrate, the bar would fill up and a party would develop. Records such as the Tom Lehrer songs were played, and I remember a vinyl of Noel Coward songs which were considered rather risqué by some of the older guests.

'I am the music man and I come from Fairy Land....' was a song often noisily sung in the bar to get everyone involved as they had to pretend to play a musical instrument. Rosemary was concerned whenever Rodney enthusiastically joined in because she believed this was bad for his blood pressure. He would go very red in the face imitating the trombone as he sang 'Oompah, oompah, stick it up your jumper' with particular relish. As the evening progressed a rather more ribald song was sung, 'Oh, Sir Jasper do not touch me' with the refrain 'As she lay between the lily-white sheets with nothing on at all'. When the last words of the verse, which had been reduced by one word at a time, to 'Oh, Sir' and, finally, to just 'Oh!' were sung, the laughter nearly brought the house down.

Ollie Maurice was a handyman on many occasions and he would produce his banjulele to accompany the singing. Once he invited his boss, the National Trust North West Agent, Cubby Acland, over for the evening who struck up on his mouth organ and the harmonious result was much appreciated by Rodney. He had previously crossed swords with Cubby over the National

Trust's policies in Buttermere, but now suddenly Cubby was always a welcomed guest at the Bridge. Ollie would also do interpretations of Elvis Presley classics, which were sometimes joint vocals with another handyman, Simon Rocksborough Smith and the song 'Return to Sender' was particularly memorable. Zoë often played the guitar and sang beautifully.

Several of the student staff celebrated their twenty-first birthdays at the Bridge, and this meant that there would be a special party in the bar later in the evening. Rodney would show his usual generosity by producing bottles of champagne. At Jen Hill's twenty-first birthday party in the bar, somebody thought it would be a good idea to see if she could be squeezed through the porthole. She took off enough garments to remain decent and then she was well-oiled (in case she was not already) on the exposed parts of her body. Several willing helpers tried to push the slim, size eight secretary through the porthole but she became stuck, unable to get her hips past the brass frame, and the attempt had to be abandoned. I have not heard that this manoeuvre has ever been repeated. When it was Rodney's birthday, he always marked it by wearing a fez in the bar that had once been given to him by an appreciative guest.

In the evenings Rosemary would generally retire early, leaving Rodney to soldier on in the bar, sometimes into the early hours. When he was not serving, he would carefully wash and polish every wine glass that came in from the dining room. Each was lovingly held up to the light to make sure that it was completely clean and sparkling. Later as he washed the late drinkers' glasses, he would nod off, slowly dropping his head onto the bar with a burning cigarette in one hand and a tea towel in the other. Someone would speak to him and he would suddenly raise his head in bemusement. This was the signal for everyone to show some consideration and retire, letting the exhausted landlord go to bed. If he was feeling less tired, he would often insist on a final nightcap for the last of those standing, even though it might well have been past midnight.

Bar games; flame-throwing

Bar Games

There were often good reasons for celebrating at the Bridge and on these occasions lively games were played in the bar during the evening. The games certainly made the evening go with a swing and everyone got to know each other extremely well. Alcohol helped to ensure that inhibitions went out of the window and Rodney expected all those present to enthusiastically join in the fun. Most of the games were suggested by the students who had learnt them at university, and some may well have come from Rodney's time in the Army. Many of them are still vividly remembered by former staff and most of these are worth the telling and are part of the hotel's history.

Are you there, Moriaty?

Two players who were blindfolded, would lie face down on the floor with their heads a little way apart. Each clasped the other's left hand as in a handshake and held a rolled-up newspaper in their right hand. One player started the game by asking, 'Are you there, Moriarty?'.

The other player then moved about before or after saying 'Yes', and the starter raised his newspaper above his head and attempted to hit the other player's head. The other player then attempted the same thing and so on. The first player hit on the head was eliminated and another took his place. The object of the game was to stay on the floor as long as possible and this was a comfortable position after a few drinks. Rodney was extremely good at this game.

The Arms Trick
This was a performance that caused a considerable amount of amusement. Ronnie Dickinson, who lived at Lamplugh, used to do a double act with Ollie Maurice. Ronnie, who was shorter than Ollie, would stand on a low stool with his hands behind his back. Ollie would stand behind Ronnie hidden from view. Ollie would then slide his arms forward on either side of Ronnie's body so that they looked like Ronnie's arms. In order to get the best effect, they would both endeavour to wear the same coloured shirt, probably having raided Rodney's wardrobe. Then Ronnie, who had the gift of the gab, would start to spin a long yarn about nothing in particular and the fun would begin.

Ollie's hands would start to move giving the illusion that they were Ronnie's. This certainly was not easy for Ollie as he had his nose pressed hard against Ronnie's back and he therefore could not see what he was doing. One hand might take Ronnie's glasses out of his trouser pocket, he would open the case and then blindly try to put them on Ronnie's nose with a lot of missing the target and several dangerous pokes in the process. By now the audience was already in stitches. Then Ollie's hand might wander up to Ronnie's face, slowly and deliberately, pick his nose and then flick the imaginary result across the room. After a while Ronnie might give a sniff and Ollie's hand would produce a handkerchief out of Ronnie's pocket and, with much gesturing and loud snorts from Ronnie, blow his nose for him. Not content with his nose, Ollie would attack Ronnie's ears with his finger and pretend to clear them of wax. Mass hysteria in the bar broke out when Ollie finally moved his hand slowly down to Ronnie's crotch and proceeded to scratch it earnestly. All the while Ronnie would continue his oration as if nothing had happened, poker-faced and behaving as if his apparent actions appeared quite normal.

Alphonse

Ronnie sometimes performed a solo trick in the bar to everyone's delight. He would produce a matchbox from his pocket and then slowly and carefully open it. Peering inside he apparently picked up a small object, placed it reverently on his hand and began a conversation with an imaginary flea that might have gone something like this:

'Hello, Alphonse. And how are you today?'

Pause.

'Feeling skittish, are we? Well, I don't want any of those pranks you got up to last week. OK? Good. So off you go and get some exercise.'

Ronnie's eyes suddenly move in an arc as though following a high-jumping flea and his gaze settles on Rosemary's ample bosom.

'Alphonse, how dare you!'

Ronnie's hand moves towards Rosemary, he looks at his audience as if asking permission. There is laughter rather than any disapproval, and his hand moves closer. Then he gives a start and his eyes follow another arc, ending among his audience. He rushes over to a guest and starts looking him over, ending with peering up his nose.

'Alphonse, will you come out of there at once.'

More laughter and then a pause.

'If you don't come out immediately, I will come in and get you.' Guffaws from the audience.

Pause. Rodney hands Ronnie a particularly vicious-looking corkscrew and he advances towards the unfortunate guest.

'Oh no, he's off again!' Ronnie puts down the

corkscrew and follows his imaginary culprit towards the bar and then exclaims in alarm. He picks up Rodney's tankard and stares into it. Rodney looks suitably concerned.

'Oh Alphonse, can you swim?'

Ronnie puts his finger into Rodney's beer and fishes around. He then extracts it and looking at the tip of his finger, blows gently.

'There, you should be dry now. Well, that was a very silly thing to do, Alphonse. You could have drowned. So please don't do anything like that again.'

Alphonse apparently leaps again.

'Blimey, that was a high jump. He's jumped so high he must be on someone's head. Just stand still all of you and I'll see if I can find him.'

Ronnie moves around the room looking to see if he can find Alphonse clinging to someone's hair. He tousles a few heads in his search and then stops and declares that he has found Alphonse. He gently picks him off the unfortunate person's head and is about to put him back in the matchbox when he takes a closer look.

'Bloody hell, this isn't Alphonse!'

Passing the Orange

Some games could be a little close-up and personal. Two teams stood in a line facing each other and the two people at the head of the lines placed an orange under their chins and tried to manoeuvre it so that it was under the chin of the person behind them. The first team to move its orange to the chin of the last person in the line won. This produced amusing situations as the players juggled with the oranges, in what could be described as an intimate engagement. Players would become face to face, possibly smelling each other's breath, and necks would gracefully entwine. An orange might even find itself further down a body as the owner of the orange, desperately trying not to drop it, pressed it hard against the other person. The same game was acted out by Audrey Hepburn and Cary Grant in the film 'Charade', which was released in 1963.

Spoon on a String

In another game a player put a spoon on a string down any chosen garment and when the spoon appeared from somewhere else on the person, it was passed to the next player in the row to repeat the process. As everyone became connected by the one string, their various contortions caused some amazing wardrobe malfunctions and the bar resounded with nervous giggles.

Placing the Coin

Putting a coin between one's thighs and walking, or rather mincing, one's way across the bar was very ungainly and was therefore always a success. The idea was to finally squat and drop the coin into a pint tankard. This required good co-ordination which, after several drinks, was very difficult to achieve.

Beer Bottle Drag

A game that required being horizontal towards the end of the evening was always popular. This required one to lie on one's stomach and propel oneself across the bar floor, clutching and pulling on an upright beer bottle held in each hand. It is actually quite hard work after a serious amount of alcohol.

Cardinal Puff

Another popular game, which was liable to get several people intoxicated and at the same time it was very good for the bar takings. There are numerous versions of this game so this may not be an exact description of what was done at the Bridge. The basic rule was that someone who knew the game well played the Cardinal and a volunteer, who was usually a serious drinker, played the Novitiate. The Cardinal demonstrated a complicated procedure which involved several movements such as tapping the fingers on the bar, touching the nose or patting the head. After saying, 'I drink to the health of Cardinal Puff' the Novitiate took a drink and did all the movements once. Then he said, 'I drink to the health of Cardinal Puff Puff' and did all the movements twice.

And so on until, if he managed the increasingly lengthy ritual for the tenth time without a mistake, he was made Cardinal. Each time he failed he had to finish his drink, order another and start again. Usually he gave up early on in the game and passed it on, so that someone else could also get well and truly sozzled.

Jacks
Perhaps the most unforgiving drinking game of all. It involved four players sitting at the bar and a pack of cards. The first one to turn up a Jack named a drink, which was likely to have a strong alcohol content. Rodney poured it and then the second player took a sip, the third knocked the rest back in one go and the fourth paid for it. Ollie recalls playing twenty rounds one evening and during the game, fortunately or unfortunately, he had to finish his drink on twelve occasions. Ollie was finally beaten when he had to drink a mixture of Crème de Menthe and Advocaat (ugh!) with disastrous results.

Flame-throwing
The human flame-thrower was a spectacular display of daring that was performed occasionally by a friend of Rodney and Rosemary's. After suitable lubrication he sat up at the bar and took a swig of lighter fluid. He then held a lighted match a little way from his mouth and blew a spray of fluid towards it. A large ball of flame shot across the bar, narrowly missing Rodney and amazingly without setting fire to anything in the process. It was a wonderful pyrotechnic display that enthralled everyone.

Balancing on a Bar Stool
The locally handmade bar stools were thankfully sturdy, and they needed to be, because another rather dangerous game involved walking round a bar stool with one's feet on the stretchers. The idea was not to hold on to anything or anybody in the process. This required a good balance which, of course, was often virtually

non-existent due to the alcohol and the participant fell off, hopefully into the arms of a member of the opposite sex.

Picking up the Matchbox
Games in the bar often required the participants to be contortionists, and it was surprising that nobody was ever carted off to hospital with a broken limb. However, it was probably the considerable amount of alcohol that was drunk on these occasions that kept everyone relaxed and supple, which avoided any serious injuries. One small accident did happen, and Ollie well remembers breaking his nose trying to pick up a box of matches from the floor with his teeth. He had to sit on one of the high bar stools, turn on to his stomach and gently lower himself, holding the leg of the stool for support. He then had to lift himself up and sit on the stool with the matchbox still in his teeth. Unfortunately, Ollie did a forward somersault and the edge of the stool seat landed on his nose, causing him a considerable amount of pain as well as producing pools of blood. Zoë said that a local friend, Simon Ballantyne, was the champion at playing this decidedly dangerous game.

* * *

These highly enjoyable games were one of the reasons that the guests and student staff returned to the Bridge so many times. Older guests happily joined in the games with the young students and probably drank far more than they had planned to in consequence. While these shenanigans went on at the Bridge, in other hotels around the Lake District the guests would have been seen after dinner in their deep armchairs, slowly sipping their nightcaps and talking between themselves in hushed tones.

The Bridge was different, all because of Rodney's infectious sense of humour, his quiet patience and his extraordinary hospitality to everyone who visited the bar.

8

Service with a Smile

Because the Bridge closed every winter there were no permanent staff. The loyal daily ladies returned year after year from Lorton and Cockermouth to work in the kitchen or as chambermaids. Some of them were always asked to come back before the Bridge opened at Easter to help with the cleaning needed after the builders had been and to generally get the hotel spick and span for the next season. The Twitchins always wanted the last cook to return for another season if she had been satisfactory, and during the winter they advertised for several students to be waitresses or help in the kitchen. The handyman's job was often more easily filled by the sons of relatives, friends or guests. The problem was that students had to return to college for the summer term, and often Rodney then had to do the handyman's job for a while, unless someone could be found who was free the whole summer.

Nearly all the daily staff worked at the Bridge for many years. There were the sisters Sybil Scott and Irene Gibson who worked in the kitchen. Then there were the chambermaids called Dot, Gladys, Jean, Lizzie and Nanny. Rodney would leave at 8 am to collect Sybil and Irene and the rest of the staff would arrive later on the bus. Rodney would take them back later in the day. After a few years this was done by Tom Rawling, the garage owner at Lorton.

Irene and Sybil were certainly the most colourful of the staff and Irene was the feistier of the two. In 2018 I met Irene, who was ninety, in a retirement home, bright as a button and she still had very happy memories of working at the Bridge, as well as some amusing memories. She told me that she worked extremely long hours in the kitchen and she rarely took any time off

The staff in 1959. Left to right: Dorothy, Marijke, Jean, Nanny, Sybil, Lizzie, Irene, Dot, Jackie, Rosemary, Brandy, Rodney and Zoë

during the day. One sunny afternoon several of the staff, including Irene, were spending their time off sitting on the grass near the petrol pumps. Rodney remarked to one of the staff, without being in any way critical, that he was surprised that Irene had the time to relax in the sunshine. The comment immediately got back to Irene and she took great exception to it. She stormed into the office and accused Rodney of talking ill of her behind her back. He tried to placate her and then reminding her that it was her birthday, offered her a parcel from himself and Rosemary. Irene opened the parcel to find a lovely cardigan. Smartly putting it back in its wrapping and handing it back to Rodney, she said, 'Do you know what you can do with this? You can stick it up your arse as far as it can go!'

In those days most employers would have sacked her on the spot. But Rodney saw the funnier side of this outburst and he let it go at that. It was several weeks before she was persuaded by Rosemary to accept the gift.

Irene and Sybil

Elizabeth Audland trained Irene up to do the cooking on her day off. Irene said that she could be working until 10 pm and then she had to be taken home. None of the daily staff drove to work in those days. Sometimes Rollo would drive the staff home, but they complained that he drove far too fast along the narrow roads for their liking. Irene said that Rollo could sometimes be quite cheeky to the staff in the kitchen, but if Rodney caught him doing that, he would be very angry indeed with him. A waitress complained about Rollo's behaviour as well; but Irene added that there were never any such complaints about Zoë.

Irene said that Rodney was the perfect gentleman and Rosemary the perfect lady. She said that Rodney was very hard working and treated all the staff with respect. However, he did like the local staff to call him 'Sir' and he and Rosemary were happy with 'Mr and Mrs T' from unfamiliar student staff. All the staff got on extremely well together and there was rarely any friction. However, Irene does remember one incident when there must have been an issue. She asked a handyman to fetch some luggage down from a guest's room. He responded by saying, 'Bugger you!' Irene retorted, 'Say that again!'

He did, so she slapped him across the face. Irene did not say if this caused any repercussions. Irene's final wages were £12 a week in 1972. Not a fortune, but she said she would not have missed working at the Bridge for anything. She added that she would not have lasted five minutes in any other hotel. That may well have been so.

Between 1960 and 1967 young Zetta Roberts worked full-time in the kitchen and she lived in, sleeping in one of the staff rooms. She remembers listening to Workers' Playtime in the kitchen while she mopped the floor. This BBC programme used to be broadcast from a factory canteen 'somewhere in Britain'. Zetta was an accomplished artist and she spent her spare afternoons sketching or painting local scenes in oil on her day off. She was allowed to hang some of her paintings in the hotel and many of these were sold to the guests. Like Irene, Zetta told a story of a young student stealing cake. However, this time several of the staff decided to lace some cake with pepper. No doubt they all listened out for any uncontrollable sneezing. Whether the culprit was found out or not, the stealing immediately stopped. Relating these two different stealing incidents makes it sound as if the student staff were all half-starved as well as dishonest. It was more likely to have been because there was a long interval between the staff lunch and the staff dinner. The dinner could sometimes have been later than 10 pm; so perhaps there were mitigating circumstances.

The daily staff took their breaks on the upstairs staff landing, smoking and exchanging gossip about the guests. They were all scrupulously honest, but the chambermaids were known to be very inquisitive when the guests had gone out for the day. They would look in the wardrobes to see if the guests had any interesting or expensive clothes and they were even known to try on the make-up or try out the perfumes. Woe betide them if Rosemary had caught them at these antics! The staff all thought that working at the Bridge was fun and they loved the friendly atmosphere. Like Irene, they would not have considered working anywhere else.

It was not until 1960 that it was decided to employ a secretary. Vanessa Ballantyne, who lived in Lorton, worked at the Bridge for three years, working six days a week in the summer and then two to three days during the winter. Her main job was to deal with the bookings and field any queries or complaints that the guests might throw at her. Other duties included serving teas in the dining room and she recalls that Alfred Wainwright came to tea one day. Vanessa rather hoped that they might have an animated discussion about Haystacks, for instance. But instead he did not introduce himself and he sat silently in a corner sipping his tea with a dour look on his face.

Jen Hill's family were friends of Rodney and Rosemary's and, in around 1965 she asked if she could work as the secretary. She lived in and stayed all the year round for two years, being treated as one of the family. One very busy lunchtime, Rodney and Rosemary were out, and young Rollo was in charge of the dining room. Lunch was served between 1 pm and 2 pm and at 1.40 pm Jen's brother and sister-in-law arrived and they naturally expected to be able to have lunch. Rollo flatly refused to serve them saying that the kitchen had already closed. Jen remonstrated with Rollo and he then proceeded to pour a pint of beer over Jen's head. Jen, while wiping away the beer that was dripping down her face, firmly stood her ground and her family were eventually served. When they returned Rodney and Rosemary, probably after seeing a damp patch on the hall carpet, were told about the incident and they agreed with Jen's decision and commiserated with her. What they said to Rollo about his behaviour is not recorded.

In 1965, while working at the Bridge, Jen became engaged and she was soon to be married. Jen wanted to stay the first night of their honeymoon at the Bridge, but she also wanted to keep it a secret. So she wrote a fictitious letter to the Bridge from a Mr Franklin, requesting the best double room for one Saturday night in September, in order to celebrate a special occasion.

Bridgettes in high spirits on the footbridge

Jen chose Room 4 at the front of the hotel for them and immediately wrote another letter confirming the booking. Rosemary was very annoyed when she found out that the best room in the hotel had been booked for only one night on a busy weekend. However, Jen pretended that she was only being kind and that there was now nothing that could be done. Rosemary continued for some time to chide Jen for her 'mistake'.

Jen's wedding day arrived, Rodney and Rosemary were invited and in their absence a regular guest, Hugo Spielvogel, was left in charge. Following the wedding reception Rodney and Rosemary returned to the Bridge and shortly afterwards, much to their amazement, the newly-weds drove up, asking if they had a room for the night. Having been told that the hotel was sadly completely booked, Jen owned up to her deception and, of course, the two were then welcomed in with open arms. This was another occasion when Rodney opened up the champagne for one and all. Meanwhile

Rodney had told the staff that on no account must they play any tricks on the couple. As if they would! They passed their first night peacefully and undisturbed. It was six months before Jen discovered that while they were celebrating in the bar, the chambermaids Dot and Gladys had mischievously sewn up their slumber wear. I wonder why they had not discovered this sooner?

The student staff lived in, either sleeping in the three-bed dormitory on the second floor or in a single staff room. In 1959, a Dutch student, Marijke Hofstra, who was at Bristol University, worked in the kitchen and she was sometimes also a waitress. I was the handyman, and such was the power that the Bridge had over the young staff, a strong friendship formed between us that is still going after sixty years. Marijke arrived before the hotel opened and she kept a diary. Here are a few entries about her duties that she has thankfully translated from Dutch into English.

Wednesday, 25 March
Yesterday I left Bristol at 8.15 am by train and arrived in Windermere at 5.15 pm after a fairly dull journey, for it rained quite a bit. In Windermere Mrs Twitchin, the wife of the owner of the hotel where I had a job, was waiting for me, together with her little daughter whom she had collected from boarding school. Right after we arrived here, they showed me the hotel. It swam before my eyes, so complicated it seemed to me. I share a bedroom with Jackie who studies geography at Oxford. I had time till 7.15 pm to unpack and take a bath. Then we had supper. The other students, Jackie and Jeanette showed me everything in the kitchen, the different types of knives, forks, spoons, plates, cups etc. They also demonstrated how to lay the tables. After supper we had to help with hanging up the curtains. We finished this at 11 pm and went to sleep immediately.

This morning I got up at 7.30 am and at 8 am the working day began. First preparing breakfast for the Twitchin family and ourselves, having breakfast, washing up and then the six daily helps arrived. Until 11 am I worked non-stop, hanging up curtains, cleaning windows, wiping, and then we had tea, after which we worked again until 1 pm. Lunch, working till 5 pm.

Thursday, 26 March
In the morning I had to do all sorts of chores. Free in the afternoon and in the evening guests arrived and my regular work began, namely washing up.

My daily tasks in the hotel were: 7.15 am preparing grapefruits, helping with early morning teas, making toast for the staff. Our breakfast at 8 am. Then making toast for the guests. Until 8.45 am until usually 10.30 am washing up breakfast. Then tea with the staff (six daily helps, Jackie, Jeanette. Edward and I). Then washing up the tea stuff and scrubbing the floor. At 12 noon our lunch, washing up until 2.30 pm. Then usually free until 5.00 pm, except for twice when I had to help with teas. From 5 pm onwards clearing and washing up tea, our own tea, turning down bedspreads, washing up dinner, which I finished at 9.00 pm. Then our own supper, so we finished up at 10.pm to 10.30 pm.

So it was hard work for the students helping in the kitchen and perhaps it is not surprising that some found it rather boring work and not very pleasant. However there was always the bar available in the evenings where they could find friendship and gaiety.

Being a waitress was also hard work but at least you met the guests and got to know them. There were tedious and fiddly chores, which included washing up endless pots and pans and making pat after pat of butter. Anne Burgess, who worked at the Bridge in 1969, thought that scraping out, washing and filling up the many jam and marmalade jars was a particularly boring job. Nevertheless, she still has very happy memories of being a Bridgette. Eleanor Stiles worked as a waitress in the sixties and said she worked from 8 am until 3 pm and then from 6 pm onwards. She said that they had their evening meal, which was left-overs, as late as 10 pm to 10.30 pm and by then she was always ravenous! She felt that despite there being a house party atmosphere, she worked incredibly hard and she was always exhausted. On the other hand, Rosa Wykes worked as a waitress in 1960 and she said that her work was great fun and more like a holiday than work. She added that working at the Bridge was the first time that she had been treated like an adult.

Carrie Watling worked at the Bridge in 1962-63 as a kitchen help and waitress, where she met her future husband, David Ross. She felt that at first she was totally inept and naïve, but she was treated only with kindness and respect by everyone. There was no backbiting between the staff and she made many lasting friendships while she was working there. She developed a love for the mountains and she still has the fondest memories of the Bridge. This was only marred by one incident when she was asked to make scrambled eggs for all the guests. She was given eighty eggs and told to crack them into a bowl. She duly cracked and dropped each egg straight into a very large bowl. There were only a few eggs left to crack when she dropped a bad egg into the bowl, so contaminating all of them. There were no histrionics and there were no scrambled eggs for breakfast that morning. Carrie was belatedly told that you first cracked each egg into a small bowl one at a time to check that it was fresh.

Barbara (aka Pomme) Frost's parents had stayed at the Bridge in 1959, and Rodney had told them that waitresses were needed. So, the next year Pomme worked there every Easter and summer holidays for five years and she became well-known and very popular with everyone. The first Easter she worked there, she arrived two weeks before the hotel opened and worked fiendishly hanging curtains, putting down carpets and deep cleaning everywhere. The day before the hotel opened, she was staggering, probably exhausted, across the hall with a huge bundle of laundry. She could not see where she was going, and someone had left a bucket full of dirty water in front of the office. The inevitable happened and Pomme literally kicked the bucket. She amazingly managed to save the clean laundry from falling on to the liquid mess on the floor, but there was a very large stain on the carpet. She set to and scrubbed the offending area several times praying that, as the hotel opened the next day, the stain would disappear. It refused to do so. Rodney was summoned and he calmly said that he would think of something. In the end he found a carpet runner that completely covered the stain and the result was a colourful carpet in front of the office to welcome guests as they booked in. Everyone thought that it was a great improvement and the carpet stayed there until it was worn out many years later.

Like several students who worked at the Bridge, Pomme also celebrated her twenty-first birthday there. Rodney and Rosemary gave her an atlas and Dorothy Fell, the cook gave her a copy of her favourite recipe book. Such was Pomme's popularity that several of the guests gave her a present as well.

As there were always young students at the Bridge, there were many occasions to celebrate such as birthdays, engagements and even weddings and the ensuing honeymoons. The champagne always flowed, and party games were played in the bar into the early hours. The hotel certainly had a romantic feel which was probably due to the gorgeous setting and the very happy atmosphere Rodney and Rosemary created.

9

A Man for All Reasons

After a few years at the Bridge, Rodney was extremely tired and he realised that there were too many jobs that could only be done by him and he desperately needed some extra help. Guest numbers were increasing healthily, so everything from shoe polishing to dealing with the rubbish was taking longer. Tourism in the valley had risen considerably which also meant that the sale of petrol had become more time-consuming. Rodney found that there were simply not enough hours in the day, and he decided to employ a young man who could do the practical jobs. Rodney did not advertise for handymen as he always preferred to ask some young men that he knew already. However he did not always have much idea of their abilities, so some handymen were callow youths with few practical skills.

In the fifties the handyman had his return fare paid (usually to Keswick station), his accommodation, and £5 a week. There was one day off a week and he was expected to work long hours on the other six days. Tips were shared out scrupulously between all the staff and in the late fifties they probably each received an additional £2 a week. On the handyman's first day Rodney would explain all his duties carefully with some practical demonstrations. After that a tap on the office door would usually get a helpful answer to a query, but handymen were expected to use their own initiative and not bother Mr T too often. Too many helpless questions and the handyman would still get a kindly worded answer, but this could be tinged with light sarcasm. The daily staff were always willing to offer advice, particularly if the handyman was friendly and good looking.

Simon Rocksborough Smith serving petrol to Ronnie Dickinson

The handyman's day often started with a monumental hangover and always at the painful hour of 6 to 6.30 am. The first job was to riddle and clear the ash from the Aga and then the two boilers had the same treatment before filling all of them up with coke. One boiler was in the drying room near the bar. As it rained a great deal in the Lakes, guests would return from a day's walking and then discard copious quantities of sodden clothes and boots onto racks in the drying room. The room therefore had to be kept at a high temperature and the result was a rather disgusting damp fug that smelled of body odour. The other boiler was housed near the still-room. Rodney called one boiler 'Bloody Mary' and the other 'The Sphinx', because it had a difficult riddle. Both were responsible for heating the water and one provided some central heating in the front of the hotel.

Simon Rocksborough Smith recalls that, despite Rodney's training, soon after starting as a handyman he did not get the boilers nearly hot enough. The guests all arrived back after a wet and windy day on the fells anticipating a nice hot bath, but they found that the water was stone cold. There must have been some very unhappy, and possibly very dirty guests who complained to Rodney later that evening. Simon was then patiently given a lecture by Rodney on how to ensure that the water in future was really piping hot. So the next day Simon was not going to be caught out again and he piled on the coke and opened up the flues. The guests duly returned from the fells, and those lucky enough to get to a bathroom first were really looking forward to a hot bath. They were in for a surprise. Having stepped out of their clothes, they turned on the hot taps expecting the promised stream of hot water. Instead, only a cloud of scalding steam poured out and they had to beat a hasty retreat. Simon had been over zealous this time and Rodney now had to give him some more training on how to keep the boilers at the correct temperature.

Both boilers had to be attended regularly during the day, but more importantly there was the commercial Aga in the kitchen. This was virtually the only source for cooking and woe betide the handyman that let it run slow, or even worse, let it go out. The cook would keep an eagle eye on it and summon the handyman if there was any suggestion that it was not being looked after properly. The ashes had to be regularly removed and once an absent-minded handyman put a bucket of hot ashes on the kitchen floor. It burnt a nice round hole in the floor covering, much to the horror of the kitchen staff. When Rodney was told he remained remarkably calm, which was his usual reaction to any misdemeanours by the staff. Mind you, he probably would not have let the offender forget it for a while. And for that matter, neither would Rosemary.

After dealing with the boilers and the Aga, the next job according to one handyman, was to take out the bread dough that had been made the night before and kept in the fridge overnight. He then had to shape it into balls for rolls and put these in the bottom of the

Aga to rise. He admitted that he never washed his hands before doing this, which might have added a certain grittiness to the rolls.

Now Rodney had to be given his early morning tea and sometimes, depending on the handyman's relationship with Brandy, Rodney and Rosemary's dog, the dog got a saucer of tea as well. Rodney liked six spoonfuls of sugar in his tea, but Simon wisely considered, even in those days, that this was bad for his health. He gradually reduced the amount and Rodney did not apparently notice it; but Simon did not dare to go under three spoonfuls of sugar.

At about 7 am the student waitressing staff would be woken in their attic dormitory. Tim Cartmell, well remembers going in and pulling off their bedclothes each morning, no doubt to moans if they were asleep and yells if they were awake. I and other handymen do not recall having had that pleasurable duty. Tim obviously liked other people's bedrooms, as one night he managed to sleep walk into a guests' bedroom. He did not describe to me the reaction of the occupants, but I hope that he did not pull their bedclothes off as well.

Then the guests' shoes had to be cleaned. These were put outside their rooms the night before and in the morning the handyman collected the shoes and chalked the room number on the soles and put them in a basket to be carried down to a mean little workroom reserved for this job. If the hotel was busy there could be fifteen or more pairs of shoes to clean. Chris Metcalfe-Gibson remembers, after a very heavy night in the bar, he forgot to mark the shoes with the room numbers as he collected them up. After cleaning them he realised that he could not remember which shoes had been outside which rooms. So, in desperation he lined them all up in the hall for the guests to come downstairs in their stockinged feet and select their shoes before going into the dining room for breakfast.

I remember one breakfast in the staff room when there was a shortage of students for waitressing, so an older lady who had regularly worked in local hotels was employed and she was sitting with us. I told those present with a grin on my face that, with rather blurred vision that morning, I had inadvertently put black polish on to a brown pair of shoes. On hearing this she announced to us that she had put these shoes outside a room that was empty the evening before, so that I would clean them for her. This wiped the grin off my face. She already had not made herself very popular with the other staff and this behaviour immediately made her even less so. Not surprisingly she did not then complain that her shoes had received the wrong coloured polish and I privately felt that her shoes deserved the treatment they received

After breakfast the handyman sometimes helped with the washing up. Then several guests would be ready to leave, and the handyman lugged their luggage to their cars. Later many coke-hods had to be filled up and the rubbish collected up and burned. The empty bins that had contained food waste were washed out in the beck. Soon after the Twitchins arrived they bought two pigs called Butter and Crumb, named after the two lakes. They were kept at the bottom of the garden and ate a lot of the food waste. After they were fattened up they were not replaced, and Mike Kyle at Syke Farm then took the waste for his pigs. Dealing with the rubbish was quite a long job as there was too much for the infrequent municipal rubbish collection.

One hot summer's day Simon just could not get some rather wet rubbish to burn in the car park. He struggled all morning and at last at lunchtime he got it to smoulder. Encouraging clouds of acrid smoke increasingly billowed into the air and Simon sat back thinking that his mission had been accomplished. It was not long before a frantic Rodney appeared to say that the dining room windows had been wide open, and that dense smoke had completely filled the room. The diners, who were choking profusely from the fumes, had to leave their half-eaten lunch until the smoke had cleared.

Until the electricity came to Buttermere the petrol at the pumps had to be pumped by hand. This was hard

Simon burning the hotel rubbish

work and the handyman was summoned whenever a car drew up to the pumps. Often it was pouring with rain and one handyman admitted that in order to retreat into the dry as soon as possible, his change was sometimes approximate. In the early sixties one pump had Regent Supreme petrol at 5/1d per gallon and the other pump had Regent Super at 4/11d per gallon, so a lot of change was needed. Motorists could also have a shot or two of Carburol (or was it Redex) lubricant in their fuel tank.

There was a system of bell rings so that staff could identify whether petrol or someone in the office was required. There was a notice near the petrol pumps asking drivers to ring the bell three times for service. It was assumed that guests would not be so rude as to ring the bell outside the office more than twice, so the notice there asked guests to ring once. If Rodney or Rosemary were needed and they were in the flat, staff could in an emergency ring the bell outside the office four times. Life at the Bridge was always interspersed with the odd practical joke and Simon would sometimes lurk near the petrol pumps and suddenly appear, stopping the driver ringing the bell more than once. If neither Rodney nor Rosemary were in the office, a member of staff would hear the one ring and rush to the office only to find that there was no one waiting. Mind you, the staff did play a practical joke on Simon. One day he could not understand why the petrol pump was not delivering any fuel. He walked round the pump scratching his head and it was not until he saw a row of grinning faces at the kitchen window that he realised someone had turned off the electricity supply.

Simon admits that sometimes accidents did happen. Once he had been stung by a wasp dealing with the hotel rubbish and this had caused quite a bad reaction, making him feel ill. Soon after this he was serving petrol to a customer with a Land Rover. It was a model where one lifted the front passenger seat and the petrol tank was underneath. He placed the nozzle in the tank and started to fill it. Unfortunately, at that moment a wasp flew dangerously close to Simon's ear, and in a panic, he waved his arms about to shoo the wasp away. In doing so he accidently lifted the nozzle out of the tank, and he poured a copious amount of petrol into the foot well. There was a great deal of mopping up to be done but there was still a very strong smell of petrol left in the vehicle. The driver, who no doubt was not very pleased, was warned that on no account should he smoke on the way home. Simon was in the doghouse again.

Serving petrol eventually became an important part of the handyman's job as well as an important part of the hotel's income. Cars were not as economical as they are today, and after they had been driven over Honister Pass their petrol gauge needles would have dropped dramatically. Worried that they might run out of petrol before Cockermouth or Keswick, drivers were often delighted to find petrol pumps in Buttermere. Soon bank holiday traffic was almost nose to tail as the beauty of Buttermere was being extolled in the Sunday newspaper colour supplements. Ollie Maurice had a busy day one May bank holiday in the sixties and by the time the guests were in the dining room for dinner he had sold a record £99 worth of petrol, which was about 400 gallons. After a quiet word with Rodney an announcement was made to the guests that another sale of petrol would make the sales reach the amazing total of £100. Such was the feeling of goodwill among the guests that one of them at once left his meal to oblige. A few years later Tim Cartmell remembers selling over £100 of petrol on a May bank holiday. He was rewarded by Rodney with an extra pint of beer.

Ollie Maurice first stayed at the Bridge with his parents in 1962 and he was impressed with Rodney and Rosemary's warm welcome, their relaxed characters and their genuine friendliness to both the staff and the guests. Ollie asked if he could work as a handyman later that year and he eventually worked at the Bridge nine times, which must be a record. He also stayed at the Bridge several times with his girlfriend. In 1968 there was a secretary at the Bridge called Deborah Stanley. Ollie arrived with his girlfriend and rang the office bell. An attractive girl opened the window and Rosemary, who was standing next to her, in her most seductive voice, exclaimed, 'Oh, Debbi, it's Ollie Maurice!' Well, that did it, and it started something electrifying between them. However, it was four years later before Ollie and Debbi stayed together at the Bridge. They had dinner with a delectable bottle of Margaux and later, in the moonlight, Ollie led Debbi down to the shores of Buttermere lake and proposed to her. There could not have been a more romantic setting for a proposal of marriage. When they returned to the bar, somewhat flushed with excitement, Rodney immediately asked them what was wrong. They announced their engagement and Rosemary told Rodney to open several bottles of champagne for all the guests and staff. Rodney was never slow to celebrate such events in a very generous way and inevitably a massive party soon started in the bar with the usual singing and party games. Later that year the couple spent the last night of their honeymoon at the Bridge, shortly before the hotel closed on Rodney and Rosemary's last season.

Few holiday jobs for students can have been better than working at the Bridge as a handyman. Nearly every handyman had stayed or visited the Bridge before he worked there. So, they knew a little of how the hotel was run, they had a vague idea of what the work entailed, and they already knew the boss. In addition, there was a bevy of young female students working in the kitchen or as waitresses or as the secretary, and they were usually eager to join the handyman for walks on the fells or to get to know him better as he caroused in the bar after work.

To Rodney the handyman had a special place in the running of the hotel. He was there to take a lot of the weight of Rodney's shoulders and to be able to take over some tasks if, on the rare occasion, Rodney was able to take some time off. If Rodney and Rosemary were going out for an evening the handyman was asked to run the bar and serve wine during dinner. To do this for the first time was daunting. Although most guests were extremely relaxed, it did test their patience when the inexperienced sommelier finally arrived with a bottle of claret when they were tackling the steamed orange pudding. Before he left Rodney would help by putting out the wine that guests had ordered at breakfast. However new arrivals would have to order at the dinner table and the handyman would then have to open the cellar under the staff room floor and frantically search for a particular bottle in semi-darkness.

Some of the staff thought that the handymen were rather spoilt. They could have a free pint a lunchtime and in the early years they earned ten shillings a week more than the other student staff. In addition, they were nearly always known to Rodney and Rosemary. So, there was a familiarity with the hotel from the start and the chance of a good relationship with the boss. It has been said that Rosemary favoured the handymen and gave the female students a harder time. This does suggest that the handymen were somewhat privileged. Maybe this is part of the reason why handymen returned to work at the Bridge for so many seasons.

The handyman was expected to put his hand to any job that needed doing. There was a large tea urn in the still-room to ensure that there was a constant supply of hot water. This was difficult to replenish due to its height and the handyman was often asked to do this. He was often asked to ferry staff to or from Lorton or Cockermouth or help with some urgent repair. Even help in Rosemary's garden might be needed. By the time the handyman's day off came around he really was ready for a break and a good lie-in. However, Rodney was always eager that they should take advantage of being in the Lakes and they should take to the hills on their days off. There was little else to do in Buttermere other than to walk and climb, so that is what the handymen did.

The Handyman, His Adieu

Adieu, ye kitchen-haunting dustbin!
Ye coke-hod and ye shoes now all adieu!
For I must flee to city's fretful din.
A twelvemonth leave the handyman milieu.

To him a shovel, now to him a book,
But Buttermere to academic nook;
Thus runs the long vacation all away –
The bar by night, the coke and dust by day.
'Tis grief to part, but part of grief will bring
Desires to come again the following spring.

Now let not Bloody Mary's tears put out
Her fiery heart, nor must her parting shout
Contend more strongly with the Sail Beck's flow.

The Bridge Remembered

For she must realise that although I go
I shall return to scrape her clinker-free
And feed her yawning mouth with coke-hods three.

The sphinx will riddle all who pass her by,
Yet her bold conqueror will still be I.
The Aga, tending culinary work,
Will find there're others who'll not dare to shirk
The daily round of extricating dust
Or other hand to tend her every 'must'.

When I have gone think not the petrol bell
Will cease to give the handyman more hell;
For its clear tones along these corridors
Will interrupt his endless household chores;
And yet that answering curse will hold new charms
To those who live amid these strange alarms.

But boilers, petrol, coke and boots and shoes
I'd leave with less of these poetic blues
Were not there others, whose gay company
It is real sorrow now for me to leave.
For me The Twitchin ambience has always been
Refreshing, kind, believed only when seen.

Adieu, ye kitchen-haunting dustbin!
Ye coke-hod and ye shoes now all adieu!
These are the tears of things, and partin'
From the Bridge is such sweet sorrow. Thus Adieu!

Written while working at the Bridge,
by John Dixon Hunt (Handyman 1957-58)

10

Over the Hills and Far Away

Brandy, the hotel's cocker spaniel, was bought by the Twitchins in 1956, aged nine months. He was soon very keen to go on long walks and he took many guests and staff with him. His favourite guest was Jo Jared and when Jo came to stay, Brandy would sleep outside his bedroom, presumably to make sure that Jo did not sneak out for a walk without him. Rodney and Rosemary being very busy, did not have the time to take Brandy for walks and they positively encouraged reliable guests to do this. In fact, there was often rivalry as to who would be the lucky walker. So, Brandy had a very exciting and energetic time each summer making many friends along the way.

Brandy was also very happy to be taken on the fells by handymen. So when the new handyman, Simon Rocksborough Smith, left for a day's walking without him, Brandy was mortified. Instead of sulkily staying in the hotel he stealthily followed Simon and only revealed himself when it was too late for Simon to return with him to the hotel, where they might have been worried by Brandy's absence. Brandy and Simon continued together and eventually found themselves on Brandreth in the company of a group of walkers. Without Simon noticing, Brandy, for some reason best known to himself, decided to abandon him and accompany the walkers down to Honister Pass. As Brandy was extremely partial to snacks, he might have decided that the walkers' snacks were better than Simon's.

Despite the frantic calling and whistling by Simon, Brandy did not reappear. Simon retraced his steps for some distance to look for him; but to no avail. Simon turned back and forlornly walked over Grey Knotts, thinking that the much-loved Brandy might have

Brandy, the hotel's cocker spaniel

fallen down a mineshaft never to be seen again. What was he to say when he broke the appalling news back at the Bridge? With a heavy heart he reached Honister Pass and trudged down the road to the Bridge. Imagine his surprise, his relief and finally joy when he was greeted by Brandy by the hotel door. Simon immediately sought out Rodney who explained that Brandy must have decided to run ahead of the walkers and so arrived at Honister Pass before them. On seeing an unaccompanied dog in such a lonely spot, a passing motorist stopped and on reading the disc on Brandy's collar, had bundled him into his car and returned him to the Bridge. Simon, who was mightily relieved at finding Brandy safe and well, had to make a hasty visit to the bar to calm his nerves.

In April 1959 Marijke and I were taken by Brandy on a walk to Wasdale and back. Here is the description of the walk in what might have been Brandy's own words.

Marijke, Edward and I left the hotel after breakfast under a sunny sky and walked along Buttermere lake to Gatesgarth Farm at the foot of Scarth Gap. It did not seem long before we had reached the top of Scarth Gap and we dropped down into Ennerdale, passing the YHA hut before we climbed to the top of Black Sail Pass. Halfway up black clouds rolled over ominously from the direction of my home, but luckily the majority of them hit Pillar and we only received a few minutes of light hail.

Once over the pass we started the long but easy trek down to Wasdale Head where we arrived at lunchtime. As the sky became more and more overcast, we decided to have our packed lunches at the Wasdale Head Inn accompanied by coffee laced with rum. I particularly enjoyed my biscuits and water. A considerable amount of rain fell while we were there, but to our amazement, when we left about an hour later, the sky had cleared. We set off, well refreshed, via Brown Tongue towards Scafell Pike.

As we got closer to Scafell Pike the snow had settled and this got deeper and deeper. Large billows of mist hung down in blankets and I did not like the going at all. I became more and more doleful as I ploughed through the snow with my short legs and at one point I turned around wanting to go home. I had never done this before on a walk, but this was really more like a feat of crazy mountaineering. Then I was given the last few biscuits and this encouraged me to flounder on to Mickledore. From there the snow was thinner and the route was more rocky and relatively easy up to the summit of Scafell Pike. On the summit of the highest mountain in England we all had some chocolate to celebrate and then we clambered down the Guides' Route to Sty Head Pass.

Marijke and Edward sat on the welcoming seat by the Rescue Post and discussed whether to head for home or to tackle what seemed very forbidding, the peak of Great Gable. As my master, Rodney Twitchin, had said that he was quite sure that this couldn't be done in the day, my companions decided to show him what Anglo-Dutch relations could do. By late afternoon we were on the summit and it now only remained to climb Green Gable via Windy Gap. Once over this last obstacle we crossed Brandreth and Grey Knotts and then tottered down to the Drum House and so to Honister Pass and the tarmac road.

It was long past my dinner time when we arrived back at the Bridge Hotel having, I believe, climbed a total of more than 2,000 metres and walked about 20 miles. Yes, we were all very tired, but we were very contented with a day well spent. Afterwards I slept and slept.

※ ※ ※

Having met Marijke for the first time at Easter 1959 I was eager to meet her again. She told me that she was returning to the Bridge in June that year and I immediately asked Rodney if I could also work as a handyman again. Unfortunately, he had already taken on another young man. Rodney, bless him, told me that he could find some extra work for me to do, so I stayed there for a couple of weeks and cemented that very special friendship with Marijke. A walk in June that Marijke and I did together with Brandy, nearly ended in disaster and this time it is recorded by Marijke.

> Leaving on a bright sunny morning at 9.30 am we took the path to Whiteless and so up on to the top of Grasmoor by 11.30 am. Here we met a search party that was looking for a Sabre jet which had last been heard of over the Lake District the day before. We were asked to look out for any pieces of the aircraft and report any find. We left with a weather eye open for debris under a suddenly overcast sky with low mist swirling around us.
>
> Keeping along the ridge over Scar Crags we reached the top of Causey Pike at 1 pm, where we had lunch. To our amazement Brandy refused the usual biscuits due, we think, to the complete absence of streams or becks along the route, leaving

him with a severely unquenched thirst. Once over Causey Pike, we descended into Newlands, where Brandy soon discovered a stream, and, after he had had some biscuits, we visited the little Victorian church. From here to Little Town with Brandy on a lead to prevent any costly incident involving chickens. Apparently Brandy, normally a paragon of virtue, had been known to chase chickens in the past. After Little Town we climbed on to the ridge between Cat Bells and Maiden Moor where we decided to rest. Meanwhile Brandy amused himself snapping at those nasty black flies that sometimes circle in clouds around you on mountain tops.

Over Scawdel Fell the weather rapidly changed and it started to pour with rain continuously for half an hour. By the time we had reached Honister Hause the rain had stopped and mercifully we soon dried out in the sunshine. Here we met the local AA patrolman who remarked on the strange, to say the least, handyman at the Bridge. He said that he had seen him ten days ago by the petrol pumps and he had extremely long black hair and very strange glasses [not Edward]. We left him at 6.20 pm and walked down the Hause rather hoping for a lift to Buttermere.

Nearing Little Gatesgarth a car stopped and the driver offered us a lift. Edward caught Brandy and tried to lift him into the car. Just as this moment another car happened to pass and Brandy broke loose and, trying to cross the road, he ran straight under the car's wheels. There were several heart-rending squeals from Brandy and the car came to rest with its front wheel on Brandy's neck. We rushed to tell the driver where Brandy had finished up and he swiftly reversed. Brandy then miraculously appeared from under the front of the car having lost a considerable amount of hair, dragging a hind leg and looking severely shaken. We were also severely shaken and probably looked ashen as well. Having tried to calm the driver and explaining that it was clearly not his fault, we tenderly wrapped Brandy in a rug and we were all driven to the Bridge. We had to break the news to a shocked Rodney and Rosemary, who took Brandy immediately to their vet in Cockermouth. They returned with Brandy at around 9 pm to say, with great relief to the guests and the staff, that other than severe bruising and suffering from shock, Brandy was not seriously injured and should be fine. The vet's prescription was a bowl of hot sweet coffee to be taken at once with two pills, then these were to be taken twice a day. Brandy decided that it might be better if he did not go for a walk for a few days in order to rest and recuperate.

* * *

Pomme Frost was a waitress in the early sixties and a keen and strong walker. Once on her day off, she and Brandy were given a lift to Honister Pass. They climbed Great Gable as well as Scafell Pike and then walked down to Wasdale, returning via Black Sail Pass and Ennerdale to Scarth Gap. Instead of returning to Honister Pass for a stroll down the road back to the Bridge, they turned west and climbed High Crag, High Stile and Red Pike. Brandy obviously decided that this was all a bit too much and sat down on the top of Red Pike refusing to move. No amount of biscuits would persuade him to continue. By now it was 7.30 pm and Pomme was beginning to get seriously worried that they would not get back before it was dark. She even considered stuffing Brandy into her rucksack so she could carry him back to the Bridge. Brandy obviously sensed her concern and, having had a considerable rest, decided to go on, which ensured that they got down in daylight. It was most unlike Brandy to behave in this way, but it was a very hard day for him with a great deal of climbing.

Tragically Brandy's walks came to an end when he got strychnine poisoning in March 1965, and despite the best endeavours of the vet, he died. Possibly a local farmer had laced a carcass with strychnine in order to poison a marauding fox and poor Brandy had found the carcass first and eaten some of it. A small memorial plaque to Brandy was fixed to a rock not far from the Bridge. It simply says, 'In memory of Brandy from his climbing friends'. Brandy's life at the Bridge must have been a very happy one. He was adored by Rodney and Rosemary and he was also much loved by so many guests. He could be seen in the hall in the mornings longing for a guest to take him on a new adventure in the fells and he was rarely disappointed. As a relatively small dog he had great tenacity and he had a huge enthusiasm for long and strenuous walks. He was so much part of the Bridge and he is still fondly remembered by many staff and guests alike.

As we know, Rodney liked to have an excuse to open a bottle of champagne for a member of staff. It could have been a twenty-first birthday, an engagement or a record time up and down Red Pike. Probably because I was one of the earlier handymen, I held this record in the late fifties, but I was soon to be beaten by Ollie Maurice and Chris Metcalfe-Gibson a few years later. Ollie was paced by Simon Ballantyne, and Ollie completed the climb and back in fifty-six minutes. The record was celebrated by Rodney with a magnum of champagne, as no standard bottle was available. This feat was soon to be eclipsed by the Buttermere and Crummock Round.

The Buttermere and Crummock Round
One evening in the bar Jo Jared, in a moment of bravado, suggested that he would like to complete a circuit of Buttermere lake and Crummock Water which included summiting all the surrounding peaks. And so the legendary Buttermere and Crummock Round was born. This involved a sobering 27 miles and a total ascent of over 10,000 feet, which Jo might not have appreciated at the time. The plans were laid, and Jo and Brandy made

excursions to several peaks where caches of dog biscuits and Mars Bars were hidden for future use. Jo's attempt at the Round is not recorded but in August 1963 he wrote this congratulatory and amusing letter to David Ross, who had been a handyman that year.

> I am in receipt of a very cryptic postcard informing me that David has done it. At last, the burden of notoriety can be passed to younger and, I've no doubt, more worthy shoulders. Too long have I basked in the doubtful limelight of being the first lunatic to attempt the 'round'. I must confess to twinges of regret when the matter was brought up at the bar, and many times I have felt a bigger idiot than nature provided for, when it was mooted before total strangers at the Bridge. It was first attempted in a spirit of bravado in an attempt to wrest from the ownership a bottle of Champers and without plan or training, and I have regretted it ever since. Haven't been the same bloke since. Can't climb at speed and suffer from palpitations and what Hugo Spielvogel would call 'puffingstopitis'. So, I can only conclude that I did myself a mischief and hope that you have not suffered similarly.
>
> However, it's all yours now David and I hand you the torch. Carry it well. I will have an intense delight in wining you if you are still at the Bridge for the first week in September. I'm glad it was a member of the staff of the Bridge who finally exploded the myth. It just proves what I have been saying for years that the beloved Bridge of Buttermere is the only lunatic asylum in the country that is run by the inmates. All success in your new-found notoriety.

David Ross had attended Sedbergh School, which is surrounded by fells, and so has a tradition of fell running. After he left the school, David continued to be sporting and remained very fit. Before he completed the Round, he did a recce and he also left caches of Mars Bars on Scarth Gap and Honister Pass. There were no dog biscuits this time, as he had sensibly decided not to take Brandy on such a gruelling route. He later started the full round at 8 am and he said that he ran for most of the circuit. Rodney, who had promised him a bottle of champagne on his return, carefully timed him and eagerly awaited his return, thinking that it would be in the evening. In fact, it was 3.23 pm when he arrived back at the Bridge in remarkably good condition for the feat he had just accomplished. Rodney declared that the time of 7 hours and 23 minutes deserved a magnum of champagne rather than just a bottle. When this could not be found, Rodney with his usual generous character, opened a Jeroboam (four bottles) of the finest vintage instead. This was consumed in the bar by guests and staff alike. Twenty-seven years later David repeated the Round, but this time it took him over twelve exhausting hours with no champagne to revive him on his return.

David Ross's plan of the Round before he completed it in 1963.

	Miles	Ascent (ft)	Hours
Whiteless Pike	1¾	1,800	0:35
Wandope	2¾	2,300	0:45
Grasmoor	4	2,730	1:00
Whiteside	7	3,480	1:40
Melbreak	11	4,880	2:40
Red Pike	14	6,880	3:40
High Stile	14¼	7,230	3:50
High Crag	15¼	7,310	4:00
Haystacks	17	7,860	4:30
Fleetwith Pike	19¼	8,560	5:10
Dale Head	22¼	9,860	6:00
Hindscarth	23½	10,100	6:15
Robinson	25	10,650	6:35
Buttermere	27½	10,700	7:00

John Scadding with the magnum of champagne after completing the Round in 1970

In 1970 John Scadding was an occasional handyman at the Bridge. Coming from London he soon developed an obsession for fell walking and he did the Round in 7 hours 43 minutes. To celebrate this achievement Rodney, of course, opened a magnum of champagne which was shared by everyone in the bar that evening. John was the only other person to complete the Round during the time the Twitchins owned the Bridge.

Epilogue

During the twenty years that the Twitchins kept the Bridge, there were no significant alterations to the hotel. Whenever guests arrived for another stay, they could rest assured that the rooms would be little changed, the daily staff would be familiar, and that Rodney and Rosemary would give them the same enthusiastic welcome.

However, Rodney began to feel the effects of his relentless hard work during the many years that they had owned the hotel, and in 1971 they decided that they should plan for their retirement. Their son Rollo was not going to take over the management of the Bridge and if they sold it, they would need somewhere to live. At an auction the same year they bought Moss Cottage, a delightful but rundown cottage in Loweswater with a magnificent view over Melbreak. By 1972, Rodney was suffering with respiratory problems and he was feeling exhausted. New fire regulations meant that expensive building work needed to be carried out and the decision was made that spring to put the Bridge on the market.

Those who had stayed or worked at the Bridge were horrified when they heard the news. They loved the relaxed and happy feeling that the Bridge always offered, the warm friendships that Rodney and Rosemary made with their guests and staff alike, the gaiety in the bar and the reasonable prices that had always been charged for the drinks and the accommodation. They could not imagine the Bridge with any other owners.

Many previous guests made a special effort to stay for the Twitchins' last season and there must have been tearful scenes when these guests said goodbye beside the stone bridge in front of the hotel. The hotel was

Rodney and Rosemary relaxing

bought by the Stewart family and the sale included much of the furniture and other contents. However, Rodney and Rosemary generously gave many treasured objets d'art and paintings to past staff. When they moved out in 1972, Moss Cottage was still being renovated so a friend, Robert Ponsonby, offered them Cragg Cottage just up the road from the hotel, and they lived there for six months until Moss Cottage was ready for them.

Once they had moved in, Moss Cottage had a constant stream of visitors who were former staff and guests. These visits were times for happy reminiscences and friendship. Then in 1985 Rodney became ill and to everyone's concern was diagnosed with emphysema.

Epilogue

He was seventy-three when he died suddenly in 1988 and his ashes were scattered on Rannerdale Knotts. Rosemary stayed on in Moss Cottage alone until she needed to go into a nursing home in Caldbeck, where she died in 2009 aged ninety-two. The family kept Moss Cottage and Zoë and her husband Hugo moved there in 2017.

Recently I spoke to John Richardson who has owned the Fish Inn since 1968. I asked him what he remembered about the Bridge and the Twitchins. He said that the Bridge was amazing, and it was beautifully run with high class clientele. Rodney and Rosemary were posh, but he genuinely admired their management which meant that the guests kept returning again and again. He, like the Twitchins, had started in the hotel trade as an amateur and they had all made a success of their hotel businesses.

What a wonderful tribute to a special couple who achieved so much by creating this unforgettable hotel.

Index

(page numbers in **bold** indicate illustrations)

Acland, Cubby 63, 64
Adrian, Lord 39
Audland, Elizabeth 43, 47, 62, 74
Badrock, Sandy 5
Ballantyne, Simon 71, 99
Bateman, Charlie 31, 48, 59
Bewcher, Giff 48
Brandy 85, 93, 94, 96, 97, 98, 99, 101, **51, 57, 73, 94**
Bridgettes 18, 79, **77**
Burgass, Elsie 34, 35
Burns sisters 7
Cartmell, Anne née Burgess IX, 79
Cartmell, Tim IX, 35, 37, 85, 89
Chercowski, Dr 60, **61**
Clark, Mary 8
Clark, Syd 8, 9, 26, 45
Coales, John 15, 59
Coales, Martin 15
Coales, Thea 16, 59
Cockermouth Mountain Rescue 16
Cockshott, Peter IX
Cooper, Mrs 10
Cowen, Zetta née Roberts IX, 75, **54, 55**
Dickinson, Ronnie 66, 67, 68, **83**
Dot, chambermaid 19, 72, 78, **73**
Ella, Eleanor née Stiles IX, 79
Fell, Dorothy IX, 47, 81, 48, **53, 54, 57, 73**
Fish Hotel 7, 11, 12, 27, 62, 105, **XIII**

Folders at Wilkinsyke Farm 7
Frost, Barbara (Pomme) IX, 80, 81, 98, **53, 54, 55**
Gibson, Irene IX, 39, 49, 50, 72, 73, 74, 75, **54, 73, 74**
Gibsons at Syke Farm 48
Gijswijt, Marijke née Hofstra IX, 78, 94, 95, 96, **73**
Gladys, chambermaid 19, 72, 78
Greenhow, Chris 7
Greenhow, Nellie 7
H and C 35
Happold, Frederick 34
Harbottle, Gwen 33
Harbottle, Stephen 33
Hill, Bunny 37
Hill, Joselyn 37
Hill, Rowan 37
Hudson, Vanessa née Ballantyne IX, 76, **57**
Hunt, John Dixon IX, 92
Iredale, Tim 61
Jackie, waitress 78, 79, **73**
Jackson, Robbie 7, 47
Jared, Jo 35, 36, 40, 93, 99, 100
Jean, chambermaid 72, **73**
Jeanette, waitress 78, 79
Kyle, Ann IX, 39
Kyle, Mike 39, 48, 86
Littlewood, Mr and Mrs 33
Lizzie, chambermaid 72, **54, 58, 73**
Lodge, Neville 34
Lovelock, Mr 33
Maurice, Debbi née Stanley IX, 89

Maurice, Oliver (Ollie) IX, 50, 63, 64, 66, 67, 70, 71, 89, 99
Metcalfe-Gibson, Chris IX, 85, 99
Morgan, Gwilym 36, 37
Moss Cottage 103, 104, 105
Muffet 62, 63
Nanny, chambermaid 72, **73**
Nelson, John 10
Noel-Baker, Philip 39
Odilia, waitress **53, 54**
O'Shea, Tessie 20
Parsons, Mr and Mrs 34
Peck, Dr Arthur 34
Ponsonby, Robert 63, 104
Prince 30, 36, 37, **30**
Pringle, Dick 26
Rawling, Tom 21, 72
Richardson, John IX, 105
Richardsons, Seathwaite 48
Rocksborough Smith, Simon IX, XI, 64, 83, 84, 85, 86, 88, 93, 94, **83, 87**
Ross, Carrie née Watling IX, 28, 80, **30**
Ross, David IX, 80, 100, 101
Rowe, Jane née Cockshott IX
Scadding, John IX, 41, 63, 102, **102**
Scott, Sybil 72, **54, 57, 73, 74**
Seascale Riding School 40
Sheila, cook 49, **57**
Shield, Heather IX
Size, Nicholas 10, 11
Sleap, Jonathan 10
Somerville, Rosa née Wykes IX, 80
Spielvogel, Hugo 38, 39, 77, 100
Steer, Alison née Coales IX, XI, 59
Taylor, Jen née Hill IX, 19, 28, 49, 64, 76, 77, 78
Thomson, Hugo IX, 105
Thomson, Zoë née Twitchin IX, XII, 11, 20, 21, 30, 31, 36, 50, 63, 64, 71, 74, 105, **30, 51, 73**

Twitchin, Rodney **18, 42, 51, 52, 56, 73, 104**
  Army career 2, 3, 4, 27, 65
  birth 1
  civilian career 1, 5
  death 105
  early mornings 19, 85
  engagement to Rosemary 3
  first impression of Rosemary 1
  love of music 29, 30
  marriage 4
  retirement 103
  sense of humour 27, 36, 40, 41, 71, 73
  tiredness 27, 28, 64, 82, 103
  troubleshooting 21, 22, 24, 49, 81
Twitchin, Rollo XI, 11, 30, 31, 74, 76, 103, **51**
Twitchin, Rosemary **18, 42, 73, 104**
  art classes 30
  birth 1
  career 2, 3, 4
  death XI, 105
  engagement to Rodney 3
  flower arranging 17, 24, 59
  gardening 25, 26
  housekeeping 24
  love of music 25, 29
  marriage 4
  retirement 103
  secretarial work 19, 24, 29
van Rees, Jaap 37, 38, 39
van Rees, Tilly née Metcalfe-Gibson IX, 38
Vickers, Maud IX, 9
Wainwright, Alfred 39, 76
Weaver, Dennis 33
Weaver, Ness 33
White Mr 41
White, Reverend Geoffrey 8

Printed in Great Britain
by Amazon